Roman Catholic/Lutheran Joint Commission

THE MINISTRY IN THE CHURCH

CHARIS ECUMENICAL CENTER
Concordia College
MOORHEAD, MINNESOTA 56560

Published by
The Lutheran World Federation, Geneva
1982

Parallel issue in German:

Das Geistliche Amt in der Kirche
(Verlag Bonifatius-Druckerei Paderborn/Verlag Otto Lembeck
Frankfurt am Main, 1981)

Copyright 1982
Lutheran World Federation
Printed in Switzerland by Imprimerie La Concorde, Lausanne

Contents

A. THE MINISTRY IN THE CHURCH

Preface 1
Introduction 3

1. The Saving Act of God Accomplished Through Jesus Christ in the Holy Spirit

    1.1 Salvation once for all 5
    1.2 The Communication of Salvation in History 6

2. The Ordained Ministry in the Church

    2.1 Apostolic Origin and Missionary Openness 8
    2.2 The Christological and Pneumatological Dimension 9
    2.3 Ministry and Community 10
    2.4 The Function of the Ministry 12
    2.5 Sacramental Nature of Ordination 14
    2.6 Uniqueness of Ordination 16

3. The Various Forms of Ministry

    3.1 Historical Development 17
    3.2 The Theological Distinction between Episcopate and Presbyterate, i.e., between Bishop and Pastor 20
    3.3 Teaching Ministry and Teaching Authority 21
    3.4 The Problem of Apostolic Succession 23
    3.5 The Episcopal Ministry and Service for the Universal Unity of the Church 26

4. Mutual Recognition of Ministries

    4.1 Present Situation 28
    4.2 Future Possibilities 30

    List of Signatories 32

B. DOCUMENTATION OF ORDINATION LITURGIES
compiled by D. Frieder Schulz

Introduction	35
Bibliography	37
Synopsis of Ordination Liturgies	38
Notes on the Character of the Ordination Liturgies	42
Main Texts from the Lutheran Ordination Liturgies	43
Ordination of Priests According to the Roman Pontifical	61
Induction into the Parish Ministry in the Lutheran Churches	71
Induction into the Episcopal Office in the Lutheran Churches	72
Ordination of a Bishop According to the Roman Pontifical	73
Literature on Ordination Liturgies	86

C. SUPPLEMENTARY STUDIES

1. Admission of Women to the Ministry
by Hervé Legrand OP and John Vikström

I. Position of the Lutheran Churches and the Roman Catholic Church	88
A. Norm	90
B. Doctrinal Foundations of the Norm	90
C. Doctrinal Authority of this Statement	91
II. Most Important Theological References for Dealing with this Issue	91
A. Appeal to Scripture	92
B. Appeal to Tradition	96
C. Symbolic Representation of Christ in his Ministers	98
III. Ordination of Women: A Question which Goes far Beyond the Theology of Ministry	100
A. Status and Role of Scripture and Tradition	100
B. Connection of Creation and Eschatology	101
C. Connection of Christology and Pneumatology in the Ministry	102
D. Connection between the Local Church and the Whole Church, or the Importance of Catholicity	103
E. Place of the Virgin Mary in the Church	103
F. Importance of the Relation of Man and Woman	104
G. Historical Roots of Christianity	104
H. Theological and Pastoral Significance	105
IV. General Conclusions	105

2. One Mediator
    by Yves Congar OP

Mediator 108
Alter Christus 109
Repraesentatio, gerere personam, in persona Christi 110
Significance of this Theology 111
Difficulties, Objections, Dangers 112
Conclusion 113

A.

THE MINISTRY IN THE CHURCH

Preface

The following document differs in many respects not only from most other ecumenical documents but also from the findings already published by the joint commission on other subjects.

Even the language itself is technical rather than pastoral in character. This is largely due to the controversial questions of church orders and structures which must be dealt with in connection with the problem of the ministry.

Perhaps some Lutherans will find this document "too Roman" and some Catholics will find it "too Lutheran". This reaction may have something to do with the unfamiliarity of the terminology used by one side or the other. The theology of the ministry has been developed largely by both sides in mutual controversy. Statements formerly marked by polemic will no longer be maintained in the same way today. Some of what was once regarded as "typically Lutheran" and "typically Catholic" is being rediscovered as a shared heritage and is therefore increasingly losing its divisive character.

The main object of the joint commission has been to set forth clearly what our churches have in common regarding the ministry both in doctrine and in practice, and at the same time not to ignore the remaining differences. It was not the intention to provide a complete defence of our shared views. Neither was it possible to deal with some themes which are of importance today not only in our respective church traditions but also in relationship with the contemporary world.

Nonetheless the limited scope of the document may also be a virtue. Although the agreements which it identifies in the understanding of ministry and episcopacy do not remove all differences, they can nevertheless have momentous consequences.

At a number of places in the document statements are made in the form of a condition. We use formulae which were similarly employed by Reformation churches in the Leuenberg Agreement, such as "if such and such a thing is taught in our churches, a consensus (or a considerable measure of agreement) is reached". This is equivalent to saying that such statements can only be ventured in the form of questions or challenges to our churches. Are the churches able and willing to consider them as being consonant with the Word of God and with their respective traditions? In addition to this, are they willing to accept the practical implications? It is the churches themselves which are competent to make a final decision as to whether and how these conditional statements can be turned into affirmative declarations.

We hope and pray that this document may contribute to the unity which God wills in his providence. We therefore submit the results of our studies to the authorities of our churches, to the theologians and congregations, for their scrutiny, discussion and comments.

Lantana, Florida, 13th March 1981

Hans L. Martensen
Bishop of Copenhagen
Denmark

George A. Lindbeck
Professor, Yale University
New Haven, USA

Introduction

1. The task of the Roman Catholic/Lutheran Joint Commission appointed by the Secretariat for Promoting Christian Unity and the Executive Committee of the Lutheran World Federation is to seek solutions to problems which the 1972 report on *The Gospel and the Church* (Malta Report) could not deal with or dealt with in insufficient detail and which have been noted as in need of further examination in evaluations of that report from both the Lutheran and the Catholic side.

2. As a first result of this task a document on the Lord's Supper, *The Eucharist*, was published in 1980. It expressed a joint witness and dealt with common problems that need further clarification.[1] Now, as promised in the document on the eucharist, the statement on *The Ministry in the Church*, with special reference to the episcopate, is presented. Greater agreement on the understanding of the eucharist requires the overcoming of hitherto existing differences concerning the ordained ministry; and this makes necessary joint consideration of episcopal ministry in order to remove the obstacles in this area to a Lutheran-Catholic *communio*.

3. The discussion of these problems needed to be focused and set within limits. It was possible to deal with fundamental christological and pneumatological questions quickly as here there are no major controversies between the two churches.[2] The same is not the case with respect to the theme of the papal office, which represents a serious problem between our churches. In view of the complexity of the exegetical and historical problems connected with this theme, a separate study needs to be devoted to it.[3] Reference will be made in the present document only

---

[1] Lutheran/Roman Catholic Joint Commission, *The Eucharist*, Geneva, 1980.

[2] Cf. B. "Documentation of Ordination Liturgies", pp. 35ff. below.

[3] Cf. the various reports on the official theological conversations between representatives of the Lutheran and the Roman Catholic traditions in the USA:
— "Differing Attitudes Toward Papal Primacy", *Papal Primacy and the Universal Church*, edited by Paul C. Empie and T. Austin Murphy, Minneapolis, 1974, pp. 9-42.
— *Teaching Authority and Infallibility in the Church*, edited by Paul C. Empie, T. Austin Murphy, and Joseph A. Burgess, Minneapolis, 1978.

to the place, the significance, and the problem of the Petrine office. This is possible because the Catholic attitude to the ministry of other churches, as illustrated by the Catholic position vis-à-vis the ministry of the Orthodox churches, is not directly dependent on the question of the primacy. So, too, the Lutheran understanding of ministry can be discussed without reference to the question of the papacy.

4. We have tried in our reflections not to lose sight of the ecumenical implications — the relationship to other churches — even if the problems we have touched upon are presented rather differently in other churches, as for example in the tradition of the Eastern churches.[4]

5. The matters we have dealt with must be seen not only in the context of Europe and North America. Urgent problems are arising in all parts of the world which are important for understanding the nature and tasks of the church's ministry. Social justice, racial equality, the dignity of the individual, improvement of basic living conditions (especially in the countries of the Third World), the creation of new forms of society — all these and many others are questions related to the proclamation of the gospel. Also the discussion of the longstanding differences between our churches must be viewed against the horizon of the challenges of today and must help to accomplish the missionary tasks that arise from them. Every step we are able to take in clearing away obstacles to the achievement of community between our churches will help us better to fulfil our Christian responsibilities towards the world.[5]

---

[4] Cf. B. "Documentation of Ordination Liturgies", especially "Notes on the Character of the Ordination Liturgies" pp. 35ff. below.

[5] We are referring to the following ecumenical documents:
Agreed Statement of the Commission on Faith and Order of the World Council of Churches: "The Ministry", *One Baptism, One Eucharist and a Mutually Recognized Ministry*, Faith and Order Paper No. 73, Geneva, 1978[5], pp. 29-56; quoted: Accra.
Reports on official Roman Catholic/Lutheran dialogues:
— Report on the Joint Lutheran/Roman Catholic Study Commission "The Gospel and the Church" (the so-called Malta Report), *Lutheran World*, Vol. XIX, No. 3, 1972, pp. 259-273; quoted: Malta.
— "Eucharist and Ministry", *Lutherans and Catholics in Dialogue*, Washington, D.C. and New York, N.Y., 1970, Vol. IV, pp. 7-33; quoted: USA IV.
— "Differing Attitudes Toward Papal Primacy", *Papal Primacy and the Universal Church*, op. cit.; quoted: USA V.
Texts of agreement issued by the Group of Les Dombes, France, consisting of French-speaking Roman Catholic, Lutheran and Reformed theologians:
— "Pour une réconciliation des ministères", Group des Dombes, Les Presses de Taizé, 1973; quoted: Dombes III.
— "Le ministère épiscopal", ibid., 1976; quoted: Dombes IV.

1. The Saving Act of God Accomplished Through Jesus Christ in the Holy Spirit

1.1 Salvation once for all

6. The saving act of God accomplished through Jesus Christ in the Holy Spirit is the common centre of our Christian faith. "Lutherans and Catholics share the conviction that we owe our salvation exclusively to the saving act of God accomplished once for all in Jesus Christ according to the witness of the gospel."[6] Christ's death on the cross and his resurrection is the climax of God's saving act for the redemption of the whole world. By his death Christ offered himself once for all in obedience to the Father for the sins of the world (Heb 9: 26-28; 10: 11f.). Jesus Christ is the only mediator between God and human beings (1 Tim 2: 5). Through Jesus Christ "the world is reconciled to the Father in the communion of the Holy Spirit"[7].

7. As a result of Christ's exaltation, his saving act is valid and effective for the whole of humankind. Jesus Christ is therefore the high priest not just once, but once for all, who intercedes for his flock before the Father for all time (Heb 7: 25). He is always the shepherd who gathers and guides his people; he is for ever the teacher of truth. As the glorified one, he remains present and active in history.

8. Jesus Christ is always present in his church through the outpouring of the Holy Spirit. It is the Holy Spirit who leads us ever deeper into the word and the work of Christ (Jn 14: 20; 16: 13). Through the Holy Spirit Christ grants us salvation, freedom, peace, reconciliation, justification and new life. Through the Holy Spirit we become a "new creation" in Christ (2 Cor 5: 17; Gal 6: 15). The Spirit himself is the gift of salvation.

9. The doctrine of the justification of sinners was the central point of controversy in the sixteenth century. "Today, however, a far-reaching consensus is developing in the interpretation of justification."[8] This consensus also helps us to see the earlier attempts to achieve unity in the doctrine of justification in a new light. Consequently, we now have a *joint starting point* for the question of the communication of salvation in history.

---

[6] Malta No. 48.

[7] Accra No. 5.

[8] Malta No. 26.

1.2 The Communication of Salvation in History

10. Just as Christ, in the Holy Spirit, was sent into the world by the Father, he now sends his disciples into the world so that in his name they bring the gospel to all humankind (Mt 28: 19; Mk 16: 15).[9] The promise and the outpouring of the Holy Spirit assures the apostles that they act in behalf of the risen Christ and not by their own strength.

11. "The witness of the gospel requires that there be witnesses to the gospel."[10] The ministry of reconciliation belongs also to the act of reconciliation. Through this "ministry of reconciliation" (2 Cor 5: 18) the risen Lord makes us participate in his saving work accomplished once for all. In the Holy Spirit and by his messengers, Christ gathers his community on earth. The church is the community in which by faith the new life, reconciliation, justification and peace are received, lived, attested and thus communicated to humanity. The Holy Spirit enables and obliges the church to be an effective sign in the world of the salvation obtained through Christ.

12. The people of God called in this way is a people with a special mission in the world: "a holy priesthood, to offer spiritual sacrifices" and to "declare the wonderful deeds of him" (1 Pet 2: 5–9). Under the one shepherd this people is held together in the unity of the Holy Spirit. Thus the church, as God's temple, is built with "living stones"; it is one body with many members and a diversity of gifts. "Membership in the community of the Church involves fellowship with God the Father through Jesus Christ, in the Holy Spirit."[11] The church is the recipient of salvation in Christ, and is at the same time sent with the authority of Christ to pass on the received salvation to the world. The community bears witness to the Lord "who was put to death for our trespasses and raised for our justification" (Rom 4: 25); it offers to God the praise which humankind owes him as his due and it serves humankind in loving self-sacrifice.

13. *Martyria, leiturgia* and *diakonia* (witness, worship and service to the neighbour) are tasks entrusted to the whole people of God. All Christians have their own charismata for service to God and to the world as well as for building up of the one body of Christ (Rom 12: 4–8; 1 Cor 12: 4–31). Through baptism all constitute the one priestly people of God (1 Pet 2: 5, 9; Rev 1: 6; 5: 10). All are called and sent to bear prophetic witness to the gospel of Jesus Christ, to celebrate the liturgy together and to serve

---

[9] Cf. Accra No. 18; and the reading from Mt 28 in the ordination liturgies.
[10] Malta No. 48.
[11] Accra No. 4.

humankind. This doctrine of the common priesthood of all the baptized is amply attested in the church fathers and the theologians of the High Middle Ages.[12] The Reformation was against emphasizing a special clerical class within the people of God and stressed the universal priesthood of the baptized.[13] In both our churches, consciousness of this calling of the whole people of God diminished greatly in recent centuries. In contemporary Protestant teaching regarding the church, the universal priesthood of all the baptized is once again stressed. The Second Vatican Council expressly emphasized the common priesthood of the faithful.[14]

14. Within this priestly people of God, Christ — acting through the Holy Spirit — confers manifold ministries: apostles, prophets, evangelists, pastors and teachers "to equip the saints for the work of ministry, for building up the body of Christ" (Eph 4: 11f.). Called into the ministry of reconciliation, and as those being entrusted the word of reconciliation, they are "ambassadors in Christ's stead" (cf. 2 Cor 5: 18-20);[15] yet they are not lords over the faith but ministers of joy (2 Cor 1: 24). They render their service in the midst of the whole people and for the people of God which, as a whole, is the "one, holy, catholic and apostolic Church".

15. The doctrine of the common priesthood of all the baptized and of the serving character of the ministries in the church and for the church represents in our day a *joint starting point* for Lutherans and Catholics in their attempt to clarify as yet open problems regarding the understanding of the ordained ministry in the church.

---

[12] Among others Thomas Aquinas, *Summa Theologica*, III q. 63 a. 1-3; Bonaventura, *Commentarium in Sententias*, IV, d. 6, p. 2, a. 3, q. 2, concl. 13.

[13] Note that "clergy" is not identical with "ordination". Cf. Decretum Gratiani C.XII, qu. 1 c. 7: "Duo sunt genera Christianorum. Est autem genus unum, quod mancipatum diuino offitio, et deditum contemplationi et orationi, ab omni strepitu temporalium cessare conuenit, ut sunt clerici, et Deo deuoti, uidelicet conuersi... Aliud uero est genus Christianorum, ut sunt laici...
His licet temporalia possidere..." (E. A. Friedberg, Textkritische Ausgabe des Corpus Iuris Canonici, Leipzig 1879-81, Vol. I, 678).
"The acceptance into the clergy, which had become a privileged class, is not conferred by an ordination, but by the tonsure... All members of an order participate also in the rights of the clergy, even if they are no clergy or can never become clergy, as for example the nuns" (Wetzer-Welte, Kirchenlexikon, Freiburg ²1884, III 544f.). Cf. Works of Martin Luther, Philadelphia Edition, II, 66 (... priests and monks).

[14] Vatican II, Dogmatic Constitution on the Church, Nos. 10-12; Decree on the Apostolate of the Laity, Nos. 2-4.

[15] Cf. the readings from 2 Cor 5 and Eph 4 foreseen in several ordination liturgies.

2. The Ordained Ministry in the Church

2.1 Apostolic Origin and Missionary Openness

16. The church stands once for all on the foundation of the apostles.[16] It was the exalted Lord himself who sent the apostles into the world to proclaim the gospel. This special mission of theirs is therefore unique and cannot be transferred. The post-apostolic church must forever maintain its relation to its apostolic beginning. The doctrine of the apostolic succession[17] underscores the permanently normative character of the apostolic origin while at the same time intending to insist on the continuance of the missionary task.

17. In addition to their unique function in founding the church, the apostles also had a responsibility for building up and leading the first communities, a ministry that later had to be continued.[18] The New Testament shows how there emerged from among the ministries a special ministry which was understood as standing in the succession of the apostles sent by Christ. Such a special ministry proved to be necessary for the sake of leadership in the communities. One can, therefore, say that according to the New Testament the "special ministry" established by Jesus Christ through the calling and sending of the apostles "was essential then — it is essential in all times and circumstances"[19]. For Lutherans and Catholics it is an open theological problem as to how one theologically defines more exactly the relationship of the one special ministry to the various other ministries and services in the church, and whether, therefore, and to what extent some of the characteristics attributed to the special ministry in what follows also belong analogously to other ministries and services. Yet Lutherans and Catholics start from the common conviction that the trend towards the emergence of the special ministry which finds expression in the New Testament is of normative significance for the post-apostolic church.

18. The special ministry and the other manifold ministries in the church take shape according to existing historical structures and thus respond to the respective missionary needs of the church. Thus while the existence of a special ministry is abidingly constitutive for the church, its concrete form must always remain open to new actualizations.[20]

---

[16] Cf. Malta No. 52.
[17] Cf. chapter 3.4 below.
[18] Accra No. 13.
[19] Ibid.
[20] Cf. Malta Nos. 54-56.

2.2 The Christological and Pneumatological Dimension

19. In the New Covenant Jesus Christ is the one Lord, the one priest, the one shepherd and the one mediator between God and human beings. In the Holy Spirit he is ever present in the church to realize his word and his work. He is present through the church as a whole and through all its members. Through baptism all the members jointly constitute the one priestly people of God (1 Pet 2: 5, 9; Rev 1: 6).

20. Within the church, there is a diversity of services and charismata of the Holy Spirit which jointly bear witness to Jesus Christ, and all together serve to build up the one body of Christ (1 Cor 12: 4–31). Paul testifies that God has given the first place in the church to the apostles; but at the same time he indicates that within the manifold structure of charismata the gift of leadership also has its place (1 Cor 12: 28). In the pastoral epistles, a ministry of leadership is already clearly identifiable (1 Tim 3: 1; 4: 14; 2 Tim 1: 6; Tit 1: 6f.). The ministry in the early church developed on the basis of such a variety of New Testament starting points.[21] In continuous relation to the normative apostolic tradition, it makes present the mission of Jesus Christ. The presence of this ministry in the community "signifies the priority of divine initiative and authority in the Church's existence"[22]. Consequently, this ministry is not simply a delegation "from below", but is instituted by Jesus Christ.[23]

21. The ministry in the church is, therefore, subordinated to the one ministry of Jesus Christ. It is Jesus Christ who, in the Holy Spirit, is acting in the preaching of the Word of God, in the administration of the sacraments, and in the pastoral service. Jesus Christ, acting in the present, takes the minister into his service; the minister is only his tool and instrument. Jesus Christ is the one and only high priest of the New Covenant. When ministers are described as priests in the Catholic tradition, this is to be understood only in the sense that in the Holy Spirit they share in and manifest the one priesthood of Jesus Christ.[24] In the

---

[21] As regards the participation of the manifold ministries in the service of Christ, see Nos. 14 and 17 above.

[22] Accra No. 14.

[23] When Vatican II affirms that the ordained ministry differs from the common priesthood of all the baptized in essence and not only in degree (Dogmatic Constitution on the Church, No. 10), this formulation wants to say the following: the church ministry cannot be derived from the congregation, but it is also not an enhancement of the common priesthood, and the minister as such is not a Christian to a greater degree. The ministry is rather situated on a different level; it includes the ministerial priesthood which is interrelated with the common priesthood.

[24] See Yves Congar, "One Mediator", pp. 108ff, below.

Lutheran church, the minister has not ordinarily been termed a priest, but the purpose has been to avoid obscuring the distinction between the priesthood of Christ by which God has reconciled the world to himself and the service of the minister. According to the understanding of both traditions, the minister does not have "power" over Christ during the consecration when celebrating the eucharist, but he speaks on behalf of and in the name of Jesus Christ: "this is my body" — "this is my blood". Jesus Christ himself speaks and acts through him.[25] This ministry is therefore performed in the communion of the Holy Spirit through Jesus Christ to the honour of the Father.

22. The christologically based authority *(exousia)* of the ministry must be exercised in the Holy Spirit. The minister must bring Christ's cross into the present not only through his words and the administration of the sacraments, but through his whole life and his service (2 Cor 4: 8–18; 11: 22–33). The church's ministers must constantly look afresh to Jesus Christ and be renewed by him. They must also heed the Spirit which acts in the other members of the church. The ministers as well as the other church members are dependent day by day on the renewed forgiveness of their sins. Following the example of Jesus Christ, the ministry in the church cannot claim any worldly advantages, but must rather be characterized by radical obedience and service.[26]

2.3 Ministry and Community

23. For Lutherans and Catholics it is fundamental to a proper understanding of the ministerial office that "the office of the ministry stands over against the community as well as within the community"[27]. Inasmuch as the ministry is exercised on behalf of Jesus Christ and makes him present, it has authority over against the community. "He who hears

---

[25] Apology of the Augsburg Confession VII, 28 and 47f., The Book of Concord, pp. 173 and 177; Formula of Concord, Solid Declaration VII, 75ff., The Book of Concord, pp. 583f.; Vatican II, Constitution on the Sacred Liturgy, No. 7; Decree on the Ministry and Life of Priests, No. 5; cf. also the relation of the celebration of the Lord's Supper to the ordination in the ordination liturgies.

[26] As a sign of this availability for Christ and for the congregation the Latin Church considers in general the celibacy of priests as a condition for ordination. However, it does not understand it as demanded by the nature of the priesthood (cf. Vatican II, Decree on the Ministry and Life of Priests, No. 16). The Reformation has opposed this order in the name of Christian freedom (cf. Confessio Augustana [quoted: CA] XXIII and XXVIII, The Book of Concord, pp. 51ff. and 81ff.). This does not exclude that the Lutheran church knows celibacy as a personal call.

[27] Malta No. 50.

you hears me" (Lk 10: 16).[28] The authority of the ministry must therefore not be understood as delegated by the community.

24. This authority of the ministry is however not to be understood as an individual possession of the minister, but it is rather an authority with the commission to serve in the community and for the community. Therefore, the exercise of the authority of the ministry should involve the participation of the whole community. This applies also to the appointment of the ministers.[29] The ordained minister "manifests and exercises the authority of Christ in the way Christ himself revealed God's authority to the world: in and through *communion*"[30]. For this reason the ministry must not suppress Christian freedom and fraternity, but should rather promote them.[31] The Christian freedom, fraternity and responsibility of the whole church and of all its members must find its expression in the conciliar, collegial and synodical structures of the church.

25. The church is called to present the image of a society molded by God's recreating Spirit. This must also be evident in the form of the community of men and women in the church. Both men and women can make a specific contribution within the ministry of the people of God. The church needs the special form of ministry which can be exercised by women just as it needs that exercised by men. "Since in our times women have an ever more active share in the whole life of society, it is very important that they participate more widely also in the various fields of the Church's apostolate."[32] In this context the question of the entrance of women into the ordained ministry arises. Different answers are given to this question in our respective churches and it poses a problem that is not yet solved. In all efforts to reach a common understanding, the significance of theological hermeneutics becomes obvious. The question of the ordination of women cannot be regarded as simply a special point in the theology of the ministry, but is related indissolubly to a number of other prior theological decisions. The divergence of opinions in the churches with regard to this question does not coincide completely with the confessional boundaries.

---

[28] As regards the interpretation, cf. CA XXVIII, 22, The Book of Concord, p. 84; Apology of the Augsburg Confession VII, 28 and 47f., The Book of Concord, pp. 173 and 177.

[29] Cf. No. 34 below.

[30] Accra No. 18.

[31] Cf. also Vatican II, Dogmatic Constitution on the Church, Nos. 18, 30, 32.

[32] Vatican II, Decree on the Apostolate of the Laity, No. 9; cf. Congregation for the Doctrine of the Faith, "Declaration on the Admission of Women to the Ministerial Priesthood", 13 October 1976, introduction (Acta Apostolicae Sedis 1977, 99).

It can be said that in general the *Lutheran* churches which have introduced the ordination of women do not intend a change of either the dogmatic understanding or the exercise of the ministerial office. Since the new practice of ordination of women is spreading in the Lutheran churches, it is becoming more and more necessary to intensify the dialogue both between conflicting views within Lutheranism and with the Catholic church.

The *Catholic* church according to its practice and doctrine does not see itself in a position to admit women to ordination. Nevertheless it is able to strive for a consensus on the nature and significance of the ministry without the different conceptions of the persons to be ordained fundamentally endangering such a consensus and its practical consequences for the growing unity of the church.[33]

2.4 The Function of the Ministry

26. In the past Catholics and Lutherans had different starting points when defining the ordained ministry. The Reformers protested against tendencies in the Middle Ages to emphasize almost exclusively the sacramental functions of the ministry of the priest, particularly the offering of the sacrifice of the mass.[34] They emphasized as task of the ministry the proclamation of the gospel in which word and sacrament are closely connected with each other.

---

[33] Cf. H. Legrand/J. Vikström: "The Admission of Women to the Ministry", pp. 88ff, below. This article is recommended for thorough study as a helpful theological orientation and introduction to the entire question of the ordination of women.

[34] In the Middle Ages since the 12th century there has been a change in the emphasis of the understanding of the ministry because of an exchange of the content of *corpus Christi mysticum* (mystical body of the church instead of sacramental body) and *corpus Christi verum* (real presence of Christ's body in the eucharist instead of church as body of Christ). The function of the ministry is directed primarily *(principaliter)* to the presence of the real body of Christ in the sacrament of the eucharist and no longer primarily to the church as body of Christ, so that now the offering of the sacrifice of the mass is understood as central function of the priest. J. Altenstaig, Vocabularius theologiae, Hagenau 1517, Sacerdos: "Sacerdos Evangelicus est, qui ex traditione Episcopi accepit in sua ordinatione potestatem super corpus Christi verum in altaris sacrificio conficiendum, offerendum et populo dispensandum. Et super corpus Christi mysticum ad membra huius corporis incorporandum..."; Thomas Aquinas, Sent. 1. IV; dist. 24, qu. 1, art. 3, sol. II ad 1; ibid. qu. 3, art. 2, sol. I. Cf. H. de Lubac, Corpus mysticum, Paris ²1949. J. Ratzinger, *Das neue Volk Gottes*, Düsseldorf, 1969, 98f. Against the background of a certain doctrine of the sacrifice of the mass which was opposed by Luther, the Reformation rejects the definition of the priest as sacrificer (cf. Apology XIII, 7f., The Book of Concord, p. 212).

27. The *medieval understanding of the ministry* remained influential in the *Council of Trent* which placed the emphasis primarily on the administration of the sacraments. Yet the Tridentine decrees are meant positively and not exclusively: according to the Council of Trent the proclamation of the gospel is included in the task of the ministry.[35] The Second Vatican Council highlighted three basic functions: the proclamation of the word, the administration of the sacraments, and pastoral ministry.[36] The pastoral ministry includes service of unity in the congregation and between congregations. In contemporary Catholic theology this service often constitutes the starting point for understanding the ministry of the church as a whole; for through the word and sacrament the church is built up as the one body of Christ in the Holy Spirit.[37]

28. The Catholic teaching that the ordained ministry is of constitutive importance for the celebration of the eucharist can also be understood in terms of the service of unity.[38] The eucharist is the sacrament of unity; it is the source and climax of the whole life of the church.[39] Therefore the ministerial service of unity belongs to the full reality of the eucharistic mystery.[40]

29. The *Reformation* was critical of an understanding of the ministry as a sacrificial priesthood because this seemed to endanger the once-and-for-all validity of the high priestly ministry of Christ.[41] "According to the

---

[35] Council of Trent, Sessio XXIII, De reformatione, Canones I, XIV (Conciliorum Oecumenicorum Decreta, Ed. G. Alberigo et alii, Freiburg, Br., 1962, 720, 725); H. Denzinger/A. Schönmetzer, Enchiridion Symbolorum definitionum et declarationum de rebus fidei et morum, Freiburg, Br., [34]1965 (quoted: DS) 1764, 1771, 1777.

[36] Vatican II, Decree on the Ministry and Life of Priests, Nos. 4 and 6.

[37] Synod of Bishops, Rome 1971, Acta Apostolicae Sedis, Vol. LXIII, 1971, 898-922. Letter of the German bishops about the priestly ministry. Herder-Korrespondenz, Trier, 1969, No. 45. Joint Synod of the Dioceses in the Federal Republic of Germany, *Die pastoralen Dienste in der Gemeinde*, Nos. 2.51; 5.11 (Offizielle Gesamtausgabe I, Freiburg, Basel, Wien, 1976).

[38] Lateran Council IV, DS 802; Council of Trent, DS 1764, 1771; Vatican II, Dogmatic Constitution on the Church, No. 17; Decree on the Ministry and Life of Priests, No. 5.

[39] Lateran Council IV, ibid.; Vatican II, Dogmatic Constitution on the Church, No. 11.

[40] Vatican II, Decree on Ecumenism, No. 22.

[41] In the document *The Eucharist* the Lutheran/Roman Catholic Joint Commission has dealt extensively with the controversial question of the mass as sacrifice and has reached considerable convergence. Cf. *The Eucharist*, Nos. 56-62 and Supplementary Studies, 4, pp. 76ff. Consequently it is possible to see in a new light the Catholic understanding of the ministry in its relationship to the mass as sacrifice.

Lutheran Confessions, it is the task of the ministerial office to proclaim the gospel and administer the sacraments in accordance with the gospel, so that in this way faith is awakened"[42], and the community of Christ is built up. The unity of the church is thereby based on the right proclamation of the gospel and the right administration of the sacraments.[43] Included in this commission is the authority to forgive sins and to retain sins. For this a special ministry was instituted by God.[44] To that extent the ministry, also in the Lutheran understanding of it, serves the unity of the church and is one of its fundamental marks.

30. From this derives the importance of the ministry for the celebration of the Lord's Supper. It is true that in the doctrine of the Lord's Supper only the performance of the action according to the Lord's institution is mentioned as essential for validity and as a presupposition for Christ's real presence. The ministry itself is not mentioned. According to the Confessio Augustana V, however, the ministry is presupposed for the administration of the sacraments. According to the Confessio Augustana XIV this ministry of public proclamation and administration of the sacraments is exercised only by those who have been duly called, i.e., as would be said today, by ordained ministers. "Wherever the ministry of the church is to be exercised, ordination is essential."[45] This affirmation does not only reflect disciplinary considerations, but rather has substantive significance for the public manifestation of unity of the church.

31. Our churches are thus able today to declare *in common* that the essential and specific function of the ordained minister is to assemble and build up the Christian community by proclaiming the word of God, celebrating the sacraments and presiding over the liturgical, missionary and diaconal life of the community.[46]

2.5 Sacramental Nature of Ordination

32. Since apostolic times the calling to special ministry in the church has taken place through the laying on of hands and through prayer in the

---

[42] Cf. Malta No. 61; cf. also the Lutheran ordination formulae II, III, VII, XI, XII.

[43] CA VII, The Book of Concord, p. 32.

[44] CA V, The Book of Concord, p. 31.

[45] Statement by the Theological Committee of the United Evangelical Lutheran Church in Germany (VELKD) on the question of the church ministry and ordination, 13 October 1970, *Amt und Ordination im Verständnis evangelischer Kirchen und ökumenischer Gespräche*, A. Burgmüller and R. Frieling (ed.), Gütersloh, 1974, 73 (B 3 b).

[46] Cf. Accra No. 15.

midst of the congregation assembled for worship.[47] In this way the ordained person is received into the apostolic ministry of the church and into the community of ordained ministers. At the same time, through the laying on of hands and through prayer *(epiklesis)*, the gift of the Holy Spirit is offered and conveyed for the exercise of ministry. On the basis of such an understanding of and practice of ordination the possibility of substantial convergence between the two churches is open.[48]

33. The *Catholic* tradition speaks of this act of the church, in which the Holy Spirit works through word and signs, as a sacrament. In the Catholic church this sacramental understanding of ordination is binding.[49] The *Lutheran* tradition uses a more restricted concept of sacrament and therefore does not speak of the sacrament of ordination. Yet in principle a sacramental understanding of the ministry is not rejected.[50] Wherever it is taught that through the act of ordination the Holy Spirit gives grace strengthening the ordained person for the life-time ministry of word and sacrament, it must be asked whether differences which previously divided the churches on this question have not been overcome. For both Catholics and Lutherans it is incompatible with this understanding of ordination to see ordination merely as a mode or manner of ecclesiastical appointment or installation in office.[51]

34. This *fundamental mutual understanding* also leads Catholics and Lutherans to common statements about the minister of ordination. Ordination is primarily the act of the exalted Lord who moves, strengthens and blesses the ordained person through the Holy Spirit.[52] Since the ministry expresses the priority of the divine initiative, and since in the service of unity it stands in and between the local churches, its transmission takes place through those who are already ordained. Thus the fact that ministers can perform the service of unity only in community with other ordained ministers is expressed in this way.[53] It is also important, however, that the congregation be involved in the calling and appointment of ministers because the ministry is for the congregation and must carry out its mission in concert with the whole congregation.

---

[47] Cf. Ordination liturgies, imposition of hands during the prayer for the Holy Spirit (*epiklesis*).

[48] Cf. Malta No. 59.

[49] DS 1766; 1773.

[50] Apology of the Augsburg Confession XIII, 11, The Book of Concord, p. 212.

[51] Statement by the Theological Committee of the VELKD (manuscript of the Lutheran church office of the VELKD, Hanover, 1976), Nos. 3 and 4.

[52] Accra No. 14.

[53] See chapter 3.1 below.

35. In the *Lutheran* tradition the view is held that a congregation in situations of extreme need can entrust one of its members with the ministry. This outlook is connected with the sixteenth-century experience.[54] Yet, without prejudice to this view, in practice ordination according to the constitutional regulations of the Lutheran churches takes place in conformity with the above mentioned principles.

2.6 Uniqueness of Ordination

36. By means of ordination Christ calls the ordained person once and for all into the ministry in his church. Both in the Catholic and in the Lutheran understanding, therefore, ordination can be received only once and cannot be repeated. Ordination must be distinguished from commissioning to service in a particular congregation. Commissioning can be repeated and, in certain circumstances, can be withdrawn. This distinction between ordination given once for all and a commissioning, which is repeatable, to ministry in a specific congregation is a distinction in many ways comparable to that between *ordo* and *iurisdictio*.[55]

37. Both distinctions, to be sure, raise problems that have not yet been satisfactorily resolved on either side. In the *Catholic* tradition, the mission transmitted once for all was expressed in ontological categories in the doctrine of the *character indelebilis*.[56] The relation with baptism and confirmation, which also impresses a spiritual sign which cannot be destroyed and taken away, is thereby emphasized. This means that God's calling and commissioning subjects the ordained person for all time to the promise and the claims of God. This doctrine was sometimes mistakenly materialized. Moreover, there was often the danger of seeing the ordination of priests as primarily a means for personal sanctification. In contemporary Catholic doctrinal statements, the *character indelebilis* is again understood more in terms of the promise and mission which permanently mark the ordained and claim them for the service of Christ.[57]

---

[54] Cf. Nos. 42f. below.

[55] The complex problem of *ordo* and *iurisdictio* cannot be dealt with in detail here.

[56] DS 1313, 1609, 1767, 1774; Vatican II, Dogmatic Constitution on the Church, No. 21.

[57] Cf. the letter of the German bishops about the priestly ministry, op. cit., No. 33; cf. also Malta No. 60. The "character *indelebilis*" shows that the three sacraments of baptism, confirmation and ordination cannot be repeated. Cf. Conc. Trid. Sess. VII, Can. 9: "In tribus sacramentis, baptismo, confirmatione et ordinatione... characterem in anima, hoc est signum quoddam spirituale et indelebile, unde ea iteri non possunt" (DS 1609). The "character *indelebilis*" is also a gift of the Spirit (DS 1774).

38. In the *Lutheran* tradition, polemical reaction against the idea of a so to speak "free-floating" ministry, completely separated from the people of God, has partly contributed towards ignoring the distinction between ordination and installation into a concrete ministry. Thus the conviction has been expressed that in principle ministry and congregation cannot be separated, but must be related to each other. Yet in the area of the Lutheran Reformation general ordination, not limited to a particular congregation, has usually been practised. In the Lutheran view, the renewed distinction between ordination and installation expresses the conviction that the ministry of proclaiming the gospel is not in principle restricted in time and space, but is for the whole church. In the same way, the individual local congregation cannot be thought of as isolated and autonomous when it comes to the conferring of the ministerial office. The call to the ministry of preaching and administering the sacraments, which takes place in the name of Christ, can only occur in the context of the ministry as instituted for the whole church. For the same reason, the repetition of ordination is opposed. In the Lutheran understanding also, ordination to the ministry of the church on behalf of Christ, conferred in the power of the Holy Spirit, is for life and is not subject to temporal limitations. Thus even if one avoids the use of the concept of the *character indelebilis* because of its ontological implications, the act of ordination is characterized by a uniqueness which cannot be given up. It remains valid even if the service of a specific congregation is abandoned.

39. Wherever there exists this understanding of an ordination that is imparted once and for all and where one-sidedness and distortions have been overcome, it is possible to speak of a *consensus* on the reality.

3. The Various Forms of Ministry

3.1 Historical Development

40. Both churches distinguish various ministries. However, they theologically evaluate these distinctions in different ways.

41. *Catholic* teaching starts from the development in the ancient church. While there are differences in the ways in which the New Testament speaks about the episcopal and presbyteral ministry, it was not until the second century that the threefold division of the ministry into episcopate, presbyterate and diaconate emerged.[58]

When the area of the episcopate later on became larger, the structure of the local congregation of the bishop became internally differentiated. The

---

[58] Cf. Malta No. 55.

presbyters, on behalf of the bishop, acquired functions in congregations within the episcopal diocese which were originally exercised by the bishop (especially celebrating the eucharist and baptizing). Through this internal differentiation of the episcopal local congregation, the local episcopal ministry also became in practice a ministry of regional government.

In the late Middle Ages the distinction between bishop and presbyter was seen almost exclusively from the point of view of jurisdiction.[59] In addition it was of far-reaching practical importance that spiritual and secular power were generally intermingled in the episcopal office in the Middle Ages. For all these reasons, the relationship between episcopate and presbyterate long remained unclarified. Jerome's opinion that bishops and priests were originally one and the same also played a role and was later referred to by the Lutheran Confessional Writings.[60]

The Second Vatican Council for the first time introduced greater clarity on this point in the Roman Catholic Church. The Council tried to do justice to the development of the ancient church by calling the diocese over which the bishop presides a "local congregation".[61] Accordingly, the fullness of the ministry belongs to the bishop alone; the sacramental character of the episcopal consecration is expressly affirmed by the Council.[62] According to the teaching of the Council the presbyters in exercising their ministry depend on the bishop; they are co-workers, helpers and instruments of the bishop and form in community with their bishop a single presbyterate.[63] Yet even after the Second Vatican Council, questions regarding the more precise determination of the relationship of episcopate and presbyterate still remain open.

42. The *Lutheran Confessions* wanted to retain the episcopal polity of the church and with it the differentiation of the ministerial office[64] on the condition that the bishops grant freedom and opportunity for the right proclamation of the gospel and the right administration of the sacraments and not prevent these by the formal requirement of obedience. The fact

---

[59] Cf. Huguccio, Summa d. 95 c. 1; Petrus Aureoli, Sent. IV d. 24 q. un. a. 2 prop. 2 (fol. 163 a-b). See also Thomas Aquinas, S. Th. Suppl. q. 40 a. 4 Respondeo; Super IV lib. Sententiarum 4, d 17, q. 3, a 3, q. 5 Solutio.

[60] Articles of Christian doctrine, The Smalcald Articles, Part II, IV, The Book of Concord, pp. 298 ff.; Treatise on the Power and Primacy of the Pope, 59-73, The Book of Concord, pp. 330 ff.

[61] Vatican II, Dogmatic Constitution on the Church, No. 26; Decree on the Bishops' Pastoral Office in the Church, No. 11.

[62] Ibid., Dogmatic Constitution on the Church, Nos. 21 and 26.

[63] Ibid., No. 28.

[64] Apology of the Augsburg Confession XIV, I, The Book of Concord, p. 214; CA XXVIII, 69, The Book of Concord, p. 93.

that it was impossible at this time to arrive at an agreement in doctrine and to persuade the bishops to ordain Reformation ministers led perforce to forsaking continuity with previous order. In this emergency situation the installation of ministers by non-episcopal ministers or even by the congregation appeared legitimate provided it took place *rite*, i.e., publicly and in the name of the whole church.[65] Moreover, the appointment of inspectors was equivalent to a recognition of the need for a ministry of leadership and of pastoral supervision *(episcopé)*.[66] It was provided for in the German area through the function of the territorial princes as "emergency bishops"[67] and by the appointment of inspectors under various titles (superintendent, *propst*, etc.)[68].

43. In view of the emergency situation, the Lutheran Confessions avoided prescribing any specific form of *episcopé* in the sense of regional church leadership. Episcopacy, to be sure, was normal at least for the Confessio Augustana. The loss of this office in its historic character has nevertheless had certain consequences for the Lutheran understanding of the church's ministerial structure. The Lutheran office of pastor, comparable to that of presbyter, has really taken over the spiritual functions of the bishop's office[69] and was even at times theologically interpreted as identical with it. This was seen as a return to an earlier ministerial structure in church history in which the bishop's office was a local one. Within this context the function of *episcopé* was retained as necessary for the church; but its concrete ordering was taken to be a human and historical matter.[70] The holders of this superordinated office are at present given a variety of titles: bishop, church president, superintendent. In some Lutheran areas, where this was possible, the historical continuity of the episcopal office has been maintained.

---

[65] CA XIV, The Book of Concord, p. 36.

[66] Cf. Dombes IV, No. 2.

[67] The princes, of course, never exercised the religious supervisory function in the strict sense but delegated it to visitors.

[68] I. Asheim and Victor R. Gold (ed.), *Episcopacy in the Lutheran Church?* Philadelphia, 1970.

[69] USA IV, No. 21.

[70] "According to divine right, therefore, it is the office of the bishop to preach the Gospel, forgive sins, judge doctrine and condemn doctrine that is contrary to the Gospel, and exclude from the Christian community the ungodly whose wicked conduct is manifest. On this account parish ministers and churches are bound to be obedient to the bishops according to the saying of Christ in Luke 10:16. On the other hand, if they teach, introduce or institute anything contrary to the Gospel, we have God's command not to be obedient in such cases" (CA XXVIII, 21ff.) The Book of Concord, p. 84.

44. We are, therefore, confronted with the empirical fact that in both churches there are local congregational ministries (priest, pastor) as well as also superordinated regional ministries. These regional ministries have the function of pastoral supervision and of service of unity within a larger area. These functions are connected with the commission to preach, administer the sacraments and lead the congregation, and involve teaching and doctrinal discipline, ordination, supervision, church order and in western Catholic practice (which in this respect, however, is clearly different from that of the Eastern as well as Lutheran churches) also confirmation. These tasks are entrusted to local ministries only in exceptional circumstances. In the two churches there thus exists a significant convergence as regards the actual character of ecclesial practice.

3.2 The Theological Distinction between Episcopate and Presbyterate, i.e., between Bishop and Pastor

45. The existence of local congregational ministries and superordinated regional ministries on both sides is for both churches more than the result of purely historical and human developments or a matter of sociological necessity. Rather, they recognize here the action of the Spirit as this has been experienced and attested from the very beginnings of the church. The development of the one ministry of the church into different ministries can be understood as having an intimate connection with the nature of the church. The church is actualized at different levels: as the local church (congregation), as the church of a larger region or country, and as the universal church. At each of these levels, albeit in different forms, it is essential that the ministry be both "in and over against" the ecclesial community.[71] There is thus a noteworthy structural parallelism between the two churches.

46. The Catholic and Lutheran traditions nevertheless give different descriptions and theological evaluations of the development of the one ministry.

47. In respect to the one apostolic office, the *Lutheran* tradition does make a distinction between bishop and pastor so far as the geographical area of ministry is concerned. Traditionally this distinction has been described as one of human law. At the same time it recognizes that the *episcopé* is indispensable for historical unity and continuity. It was for this reason that after the loss of the link with the historic episcopate, a new structuring of *episcopé* was needed.

---

[71] At the level of the universal church, moreover, there also arise some special problems; cf. chapter 3.5 below.

48. The *Catholic* tradition makes a theological distinction between bishop and priest (episcopate and presbyterate). The Council of Trent held that this distinction exists *divina ordinatione*,[72] and thereby deliberately avoided the term *de iure divino*. All that the Second Vatican Council says is that this distinction has existed from antiquity *(ab antiquo)*.[73] Nevertheless, the Catholic tradition also speaks of only one single sacrament of orders in which bishop, priest and deacon share in different ways.

49. *If* both churches acknowledge that for faith this historical development of the one apostolic ministry into a more local and a more regional ministry has taken place with the help of the Holy Spirit and to this degree constitutes something essential for the church, then a *high degree of agreement* has been reached.

3.3 Teaching Ministry and Teaching Authority

50. In the *Catholic* teaching the most eminent task of the bishops consists of the preaching of the gospel.[74] In this the bishops are both preachers of the faith and authentic teachers of the faith.[75] They do not stand above the Word of God, but serve it; they have to listen to it devoutly, guard it scrupulously, and interpret it faithfully.[76] They should bear witness to the glad tidings in a manner adapted to the needs of the times, i.e., to speak to the difficulties and questions by which people are burdened and troubled. But they should also protect the Good News and defend it against omissions and falsifications. They should show how closely the church's teaching is connected with the dignity of human persons, their freedom and their rights, with the questions of peace and of the just distribution of earthly goods among all peoples.[77]

51. The bishops can discharge this task only in community with the whole church. For the entire people of God participates in the prophetic office of Christ; the entire people of God receives the supernatural sense of the faith from the Holy Spirit.[78] Priests share Christ's prophetic office in

---

[72] DS 1776.

[73] Vatican II, Dogmatic Constitution on the Church, No. 28. As regards the problem and the meaning of the term *ius divinum*, cf. Malta Nos. 31-34.

[74] Council of Trent, op. cit., Sessio XXIV, Can. IV, 739.

[75] Vatican II, Dogmatic Constitution on the Church, No. 25.

[76] Ibid., Dogmatic Constitution on Divine Revelation, No. 10.

[77] Ibid., Decree on the Bishops' Pastoral Office in the Church, No. 12.

[78] Ibid., Dogmatic Constitution on the Church, No. 12.

a special manner; they are co-workers in the preaching and teaching ministry of the bishops.[79] If the bishops are to perform their functions, especially today, they also need the collaboration of theologians. The theologians must intellectually investigate the faith by interpreting it on the basis of the witness of Holy Scripture and of the church tradition and by making it accessible to contemporary minds. For this they need adequate freedom within the church. The teaching ministry of the bishops, therefore, takes place in a many-sided exchange regarding faith with believers, priests, and theologians.

52. When controversies endanger the unity of faith in the church, the bishops have both the right and the duty to make binding decisions. On those matters where the bishops interpret the revealed faith in universal agreement with each other and in communion with the Bishop of Rome, their witness has final authority and infallibility.[80] Such infallible decisions, however, in order to be juridically valid, do not need a special formal consent by the totality of the local congregations of the faithful, but they depend on extensive reception in order to have living power and spiritual fruitfulness in the church.

53. In the *Lutheran* view the office of the bishop is "to preach the Gospel, forgive sins, judge doctrine and condemn doctrine that is contrary to the Gospel". The holders of the episcopal office are therefore entrusted in a special manner with the task of watching over the purity of the gospel, and this involves a teaching ministry which should be carried out "not by human power but by God's Word alone"[81].

54. Given the situation created by the Reformation, it was in actual fact the theologians who fulfilled this teaching function, above all in the formulation of the Confessions. Thus the theological faculties and with them the officials charged with supervising church affairs became the authorities in formulating doctrine, even though doctrinal decisions acquired legal status through the action of the territorial princes as "emergency bishops". Always, however, the binding character of doctrine became manifest through the process of reception in which each adult Christian, as receiver of the Spirit, was accorded, at least in dogmatic principle, full power of authority to judge teaching.

55. Also in our day there is interpretation and development of church doctrine in Lutheran churches through the decisions of the appropriate ecclesial authorities (synods, church authorities, etc.). A decisive part in

---

[79] Ibid., Decree on the Ministry and Life of Priests, No. 4.

[80] Ibid., Dogmatic Constitution on the Church, No. 25.

[81] CA XXVIII, 21ff., The Book of Concord, p. 84.

these is played by teachers of theology together with non-ordained church members and ordained ministers. Such decisions have the purpose of serving the contemporary proclamation and unity of the church. Yet here there appear a number of difficult problems. University theology has sometimes become remote from the life of the church. In other cases there have been doubts that there is any need for a further binding development. Even where such further development is considered necessary, appropriate means are often lacking, or there is not enough clarity about the teaching competence of existing agencies.

56. The Lutheran churches are therefore confronted with the need to rethink the problem of the teaching office and the teaching authority. The question of the function of the episcopal ministry arises especially in this connection. On the other hand, the significance of the reception of doctrinal statements by the community and the competence of the community to judge in questions of faith must be considered.

57. *In both churches* there thus exists a teaching responsibility at a supra-congregational level, which, of course, is performed in different ways. But one can recognize a certain parallelism between the two churches. In both churches, teaching responsibility is tied to the whole church's witness to the faith. Both churches know that their norm is the gospel. Both churches are faced by the question of the nature and the binding character of doctrinal decisions. The treatment of this problem constitutes a common task, in which particular attention will have to be paid to the question of infallibility.

58. Already today Catholics and Lutherans can *join* in saying "that the Holy Spirit unceasingly leads and keeps the church in the truth". "The church's abiding in the truth should not be understood in a static way, but as a dynamic event which takes place with the aid of the Holy Spirit in ceaseless battle against error and sin in the church as well as in the world."[82]

3.4 The Problem of Apostolic Succession

59. The most important question regarding the theology of the episcopal office and regarding the mutual recognition of ministries is the problem of the apostolic succession. This is normally taken to mean the unbroken ministerial succession of bishops in a church. But apostolic succession is also often understood to refer in the substantive sense to the apostolicity of the church in faith.

---

[82] Malta Nos. 22 and 23.

60. The starting point must be the apostolicity of the church in the substantive sense. "The basic intention of the doctrine of apostolic succession is to indicate that, throughout all historical changes in its proclamation and structures, the church is at all times referred back to its apostolic origin."[83] In the New Testament and in the period of the early fathers, the emphasis was placed more on the substantive understanding of the apostolic succession in faith and life. The Lutheran tradition speaks in this connection of a *successio verbi*. In present-day Catholic theology, more and more often the view is adopted that the substantive understanding of apostolicity is primary. Far-reaching agreement on this understanding of apostolic succession is therefore developing.

61. As regards the succession of the ministers, the joint starting point for both Catholics and Lutherans is that there is an integral relation between the witness of the gospel and witnesses to the gospel.[84] The witness to the gospel has been entrusted to the church as a whole. Therefore, the whole church as the *ecclesia apostolica* stands in the apostolic succession. Succession in the sense of the succession of ministers must be seen within the succession of the whole church in the apostolic faith.[85]

62. The *Catholic* church sees this succession of ministers as realized in the succession in the episcopal office.[86] In Catholic teaching the fullness of the ordained ministry exists only in the episcopal office.[87] Nevertheless, the apostolic succession in the episcopal office does not consist primarily in an unbroken chain of those ordaining to those ordained, but in a succession in the presiding ministry of a church, which stands in the continuity of apostolic faith and which is overseen by the bishop in order to keep it in the communion of the Catholic and apostolic church. Thus originates the college of those who maintain the communion of the church. The episcopal college serves on its level and on the foundation of the apostles to continue the function of the college of the apostles.

The episcopate which stands in the apostolic succession is bound to the canon of Scripture and the apostolic doctrinal tradition and must bear living witness to them. While it is possible for the individual bishop to fall away from the continuity of the apostolic faith, he loses *eo ipso*, according to Catholic tradition, the right to exercise his ministry. Catholic tradition holds that the episcopate as a whole is nevertheless kept firm in the truth of the gospel. In this sense, Catholic doctrine regards the apostolic

---

[83] Ibid., No. 57.

[84] Cf. ibid., No. 48.

[85] Cf. ibid., No. 57.

[86] Vatican II, Dogmatic Constitution on the Church, No. 20.

[87] Ibid., Nos. 21 and 26.

succession in the episcopal office as a sign and ministry of the apostolicity of the church.

63. For the *Lutheran* tradition also the apostolic succession is necessary and constitutive for both the church and for its ministry. Its confessional writings claim to stand in the authentic Catholic tradition,[88] and emphasize the historical continuity of the church which has never ceased to exist.[89]

64. For the Lutherans in the sixteenth century, the authenticity of apostolic succession in the form of historic succession in the episcopal office was called in question because it failed to witness to agreement in the proclamation of the gospel, and because the episcopate refused fellowship with them, especially by denying them the service of ordaining their preachers, and thus deprived them of the historic succession in office. For them, therefore, apostolic succession came to focus on the right preaching of the gospel, which always included the ministry, and on faith and the testimony of a Christian life. Yet they were convinced that the gospel had been given to the church as a whole and that, with the right preaching of the Word and the celebration of the sacraments according to the gospel, apostolic succession in the substantive sense continued within the congregations. Based on this, the ordination of ministers by ministers continued to be performed in the Lutheran church. This ordination remained oriented towards the entire church and towards recognition by its ministers.

65. Thus, despite diverse historical developments, the Lutheran Reformation affirmed and intended to preserve the historical continuity of church order as an expression of the unity of the apostolic church among all peoples and throughout all centuries, presupposing, of course, that the gospel is rightly proclaimed. This intention must be maintained even in the face of contrary historical developments for the sake of the faith that the church abides.[90] This point is expressly stressed in the fundamental articles of the Augsburg Confession,[91] and also by the references made in the confessional writings to church teachers of all times.[92]

---

[88] CA XXI, Epilogue, The Book of Concord, pp. 47f.; CA XXII, Preface, The Book of Concord, pp. 48f.; CA XXVIII, Conclusion, The Book of Concord, p. 95; cf. USA IV, No.23.

[89] CA VII, The Book of Concord, p. 32; Apology of the Augsburg Confession IV, 211, The Book of Concord, p. 136; Catalogus Testimoniorum, BSLK 1101-1135; cf. USA IV, No. 26.

[90] CA VII, 1, The Book of Concord, p. 32.

[91] Cf. ibid.; CA XXI, Epilogue, The Book of Concord, pp. 47f.; CA XXI conclusion of part I and introduction to part II, The Book of Concord, pp. 48f.

[92] Cf. especially Catalogus Testimoniorum, op. cit.

66. These considerations provide the basis for a Lutheran evaluation of the historic succession as a sign of such unity. The Lutheran conviction is that acceptance of communion with the episcopal office in the historic succession is meaningful not as an isolated act,[93] but only as it contributes to the unity of the church in faith and witnesses to the universality of the gospel of reconciliation.

3.5 The Episcopal Ministry and Service for the Universal Unity of the Church

67. Along with reflection on episcopacy, there naturally also arises the question of ministry to the universal unity of the church. This question can be mentioned here only as a problem. It calls for further and more detailed treatment.

68. According to *Catholic* teaching, it is primarily by preaching and teaching that the bishops minister to unity within their local churches and between the local churches. Each local church is a realization and representation of the one church of Jesus Christ[94] only in community *(communio)* with the other local churches. This is why the individual bishop with his office forms a part of the community of all the bishops (collegiality). Each individual bishop and all the bishops together are entrusted with the care of the entire church, which exists in and arises from the many local churches.[95]

69. This *communio* between the local churches and their bishops has its point of reference in communion with the Church of Rome and the Bishop of Rome as the holder of the Chair of Peter. In this capacity he presides over the *communio (Agape)*.[96] Rome is the place of the martyrdom of the apostles Peter and Paul; the Church of Rome was preserved amid the storms of persecution and in the confrontation with heresies, and played a leading role in the establishment of the canon of Scripture and the apostolic creed. From the fourth century onward, the promise given to Peter "on this rock I will build my church" (Mt 16: 18) and the commission assigned to him "strengthen your brethren" (Lk 22: 32) was applied to the Church of Rome and to the Bishop of the *cathedra Petri*. According to Catholic teaching, the Lord has transmitted to the Bishop of Rome, as the successor of Peter, the supreme pastoral office in the church. The ministry of the Bishop of Rome is to serve the unity of the universal

---

[93] Cf. No. 82 below.

[94] Vatican II, Decree on the Bishops' Pastoral Office in the Church, No. 11.

[95] Ibid., Dogmatic Constitution on the Church, No. 23.

[96] Cf. Ignatius of Antioch, *Epistula ad Romanos* (Inscr.).

church and legitimate diversity in the church.[97] His ministry of unity is "the perpetual and visible source and foundation of the unity of the bishops and of the multitude of the faithful"[98].

70. Since the unity of the church is primarily unity in the one faith, the ministry of the Bishop of Rome within the episcopal college includes a special ministry to the unity of the faith of the church. He serves the unity of the whole church in faith and mission. It is promised to him that through the power of the Holy Spirit he is preserved from error in teaching when he solemnly declares the faith of the church (infallibility).[99] In his succession to the chair of Peter he is a witness of faith in the Jesus Christ to whom Peter was the first to bear witness in an abiding and authoritative way. This is the witness to which the church must always refer (Mt 16: 16; Lk 24: 34; 1 Cor 15: 5).[100]

71. There were differences in detail in the ways the ministry of unity of the Bishop of Rome was understood and exercised in the first and second millennia. With its two dogmas of the universal primacy of the papal jurisdiction and the infallibility of particular papal doctrinal decisions, the First Vatican Council highlighted the service to unity of the Bishop of Rome, though without, to be sure, making sufficiently clear the degree to which this service is embedded in the total church. The Second Vatican Council confirmed this teaching of the First Vatican Council, but at the same time firmly anchored it once again in an all-embracing ecclesial context by its statements on the significance of the local churches and the collegiality of the episcopate. The frequent talk of the "Petrine office" in the post-conciliar period reflects the effort to interpret the papacy in terms of the Peter typology of the New Testament. This shows that "the concrete shape of this office may vary greatly in accordance with changing historical conditions"[101]. Aware as the Catholic church is that the papacy remains to this day for many Christians one of the greatest obstacles on the road to unity of the churches, it nevertheless hopes that as it is structurally renewed in the light of Holy Scripture and the tradition, it may more and more in the future provide an important service to unity.

72. For the *Lutheran* churches, likewise, it is essential to be aware of the interrelationship of the individual local and regional churches. Increa-

---

[97] Vatican II, Dogmatic Constitution on the Church, Nos. 22f.

[98] First Vatican Council, DS 3050f.; Vatican II, Dogmatic Constitution on the Church, No. 23.

[99] First Vatican Council, DS 3074; Vatican II, Dogmatic Constitution on the Church, No. 25.

[100] Cf. Vatican II, Dogmatic Constitution on Divine Revelation, No. 10.

[101] Malta No. 66.

singly questions arise regarding the visible forms of church fellowship which represent a world-wide bond of faith. The churches have learned to collaborate in practical and theological matters in various ecumenical organizations. They have come to know each other better and have established concrete contacts with each other and thus have come into a deeper community. In recent years, the ecumenical dialogue among other things has led to the discussion of various models for the unity of the universal church, including first and foremost the model of conciliar fellowship of the churches. According to this model, the local churches form part of a world-wide and binding fellowship without having to give up their legitimate individual characteristics.

73. Also in this connection the question arises for Lutherans of service to the unity of the church at the universal level. The Reformers never surrendered the view that the council is the locus for the expression of the consensus of all Christendom, and, therefore, of universal church unity, even when they doubted whether a genuinely universal and free council could still be assembled. It seemed to Lutherans that the papacy suppressed the gospel and was to this extent an obstacle to true Christian unity. The doctrinal decision of the First Vatican Council confirmed this conviction in the minds of many. While the traditional controversies have not yet been completely settled, it can nevertheless be said that Lutheran theologians today are among those who look not only to a future council or to the responsibility of theology, but also to a special Petrine office, when it is a question of service to the unity of the church at the universal level. — Much remains theologically open here, especially the question as to how this universal ministry in the service of truth and unity can be exercised, whether by a general council, or by a group, or by an individual bishop respected by all Christians. But in various dialogues, the *possibility* begins to emerge that the Petrine office of the Bishop of Rome also need not be excluded by Lutherans as a visible sign of the unity of the church as a whole, "insofar as [this office] is subordinated to the primacy of the gospel by theological reinterpretation and practical restructuring"[102].

4. Mutual Recognition of Ministries

4.1 Present Situation

74. The convergences in the understanding and the structuring of the church's ministry presented in chapters two and three give great urgency to the question of the mutual recognition of ministries. This is true

---

[102] Malta No. 66; cf. USA V.

especially because eucharistic fellowship between our two churches depends essentially on the answer to this question. The question arises for both sides in a different way.

75. Before the Second Vatican Council there were no official pronouncements in *Catholic* teaching on the question of the validity or invalidity of the ministries in the Lutheran church. It was traditionally assumed that they were invalid. The Second Vatican Council speaks of a *defectus* in the sacrament of orders in the churches stemming from the Reformation.[103] It did not explain in what sense this applies to the individual churches and ecclesial communities who "differ... among themselves to a considerable degree"[104]. Its intention, in any case, was not to take a final position, but rather to highlight a number of considerations that "can and ought to serve as a basis and motivation for such [ecumenical] dialogue"[105].

76. The ecumenical dialogue that has been going on since that time has increasingly given rise to the question whether *defectus* refers to a partial lack rather than a complete absence. In considering this problem, the ecumenical experience of the action of the Holy Spirit in the other churches[106] and of the spiritual fruitfulness of their ministries plays an important role. In addition, recent insights in the fields of biblical theology and of the history of theology and of dogma are of importance, especially the recognition of the diversity both of the ecclesial ministries in the New Testament and of their relationships to the community and to changing historical situations. In this connection it may also be worthy of mention that in the history of the Catholic church there have been cases of the ordination of priests by priests.[107]

77. In the light of post-conciliar ecumenical discussion — as also reflected in the preceding chapters — it seems possible to speak of a *defectus ordinis* in the sense of a lack of the fullness of the church's ministry. In fact it is the Catholic conviction that standing in the historic succession belongs to the fullness of the episcopal ministry. But this fact does not, according to the Catholic view, preclude that the ministry in the Lutheran churches exercises essential functions of the ministry that Jesus Christ instituted in his church.[108]

---

[103] Vatican II, Decree on Ecumenism, No. 22.

[104] Ibid., No. 19.

[105] Ibid.,

[106] Cf. ibid., No. 3.

[107] Papal bulls of Pope Bonifatius IV, DS 1145-46; Martin V, DS 1290; Malta Nos. 58, 63; USA IV, No. 20.

[108] Dombes III, No. 40.

78. The Catholic attitude to the ministry of other churches, as its view of the ministry in the Orthodox churches shows, does not depend directly on the question of the primacy. Yet for a full recognition of ministries in a reconciliation of churches, according to Catholic understanding, the Petrine office must also be taken into consideration.

79. For *Lutherans* the question presents itself differently. According to the Lutheran Confessions, the church exists wherever the gospel is preached in its purity and the sacraments are rightly administered.[109] Thus, Lutherans do not claim that the office of the ministry is found only in their own churches' ministry, i.e., they do not deny that it exists in the Catholic church.

80. If, as Augsburg Confession VII declares, agreement in the above two marks (in which the ministry is included)[110] is sufficient for the true unity of the church, then these marks are fundamental conditions for identifying church unity. The *satis* must not be understood, however, as if it somehow denied the legitimacy of further agreements. When such further agreements are described as "not necessary", this does not oppose the growth of unity in Christ even in the sense of structural unification, but rather promotes the right kind of freedom for such growth. Unification should take place as an expression of Spirit-worked faith in the gospel which — like the works of the justified sinner — follows this faith. Understood in this manner, the Lutheran *satis est* is, therefore, not contrary to the desire for the "fullness" of church life, but actually opens up the way to this fullness. One must ask, in other words, what form of church structure most effectively helps the proclamation of the gospel and the life and mission of the church. The *satis est* understood in this sense frees Lutherans to face up to the call for communion with the historic episcopal office.

4.2 Future Possibilities

81. The rapprochement between the divided churches which has been reached, the advances in ecumenical discussion, increasingly close practical cooperation between the ministers and congregations of both churches and, not least, the urgent pastoral problems which can only be solved in common, particularly the hope for joint celebration of the

---

[109] CA VII, The Book of Concord, p. 32; Malta No. 64.

[110] CA V, The Book of Concord, p. 31; CA XXVIII, 20, The Book of Concord, p. 84. The *satis* is not intended to suggest that the church ministry is superfluous for unity, because it has been instituted by God with the task of preaching and administering the sacraments.

Lord's Supper, suggest the desirability of the mutual recognition by the two churches of their ministries in the not too distant future. This would be a decisive step towards eliminating the scandal of our separation at the Lord's Supper. Christians of both churches could then bear more credible testimony before the world of their fellowship in the love of Christ. Even before the mutual recognition of the ministries has been achieved, each church should by all means take into consideration developments in the other church when further developing its own ministries.

82. On what conditions and in what way would such a mutual recognition of ministries be possible? There is as yet no generally agreed upon answer to this question. Proposals for such procedures as a supplementary ordination, a juridical declaration or a mutual laying on of hands, any of which could be interpreted as either an act of ordination or as an act of reconciliation, are not completely satisfactory if they are understood as isolated acts. Nor can the question be answered exclusively in terms of canonical criteria of validity. Mutual recognition must not be regarded as an isolated act or carried out as such. It must occur in the confession of the one faith in the context of the unity of the church and in the celebration of the Lord's Supper, the sacrament of unity. Lutherans and Catholics, therefore, share the conviction that ordination by bishops, apart from reference to specific church communities, does not represent a solution. The only theologically meaningful way of solving this question is through a process in which the churches reciprocally accept each other. From this standpoint, the acceptance of full church communion would signify also the mutual recognition of ministries. The precondition for such acceptance of full church communion is agreement in the confession of faith — which must also include a common understanding of the church's ministry — a common understanding of the sacraments, and fraternal fellowship in Christian and church life.

83. Such a recognition can only come about gradually. The various stages lead from a mutual respect of ministries through practical cooperation to full recognition of the ministry of the other church which is identical to the acceptance of eucharistic fellowship. We are grateful that today mutual respect of ministries and practical cooperation already take place to a large extent, and that in the meantime a considerable degree of common understanding of the faith, including a common understanding of the church's ministry, has been reached. For this reason it seems to us that further steps in the direction of a full mutual recognition of ministries are now indicated.[111]

---

[111] Cf. Accra Nos. 93-100.

84. A primary desideratum is as broad as possible a process of reception of the findings of previous ecumenical dialogues on the ministry of the church. We therefore request church leaders to distribute the present document to their churches for study. In addition, we ask the churches to continue to seek and to promote the cooperation of congregations and of ministers. Each church must make sure that its practice in the ordination and installation of ministers corresponds to the consensus that has already been achieved. Liturgical ordination formulae that do not correspond to the present state of the ecumenical discussion need revision.

85. If all this is done, the next step could consist of a mutual recognition that the ministry in the other church exercises essential functions of the ministry that Jesus Christ instituted in his church and, which one believes, is fully realized in one's own church. This as yet incomplete mutual recognition would include the affirmation that the Holy Spirit also operates in the other church through its ministries and makes use of these as means of salvation in the proclamation of the gospel, the administration of the sacraments, and the leadership of congregations. Such a statement is possible on the basis of what has been said up to now. It would be an important step in helping us through further reciprocal reception to arrive eventually at full mutual recognition of ministries by the acceptance of full church and eucharistic fellowship.

86. The hope of achieving full church and eucharistic fellowship is not based on our human possibilities, but is rather founded on the promise of the Lord who through his Spirit is effectively manifest in the growing unity of our churches. Such hopes will also patiently withstand difficulties and disappointments, trusting in the prayer of our Lord "that they may all be one" (Jn 17: 21).

List of Signatories

This document was signed by all members of the joint commission:

Roman Catholic Members:

The Rt. Rev. H. L. Martensen (chairperson)
The Rt. Rev. Dr. P. W. Scheele
Prof. Dr. J. Hoffmann
The Rev. Dr. J. F. Hotchkin
The Rev. Chr. Mhagama
Prof. Dr. St. Napiorkowski
Dr. V. Pfnür

Lutheran Members:

Prof. Dr. G. A. Lindbeck (chairperson)
The Rt. Rev. D. H. Dietzfelbinger
The Rev. Dr. K. Hafenscher
Drs. P. Nasution
The Rev. I. K. Nsibu
Prof. Dr. L. Thunberg
Prof. Dr. Bertoldo Weber

Consultants:

Prof. Dr. P. Bläser MSC (Roman Catholic)
Prof. Dr. W. Kasper (Roman Catholic)
Prof. Dr. U. Kühn (Lutheran)
Prof. Dr. H. Legrand OP (Roman Catholic)
Prof. D. Dr. W. Lohff (Lutheran)
Prof. Dr. H. Meyer (Lutheran)
Prof. Dr. H. Schütte (Roman Catholic)
The Rt. Rev. Dr. J. Vikström (Lutheran)

Staff Members:

P. Dr. P. Duprey PA (Secretariat for Promoting Christian Unity)
Msgr. Dr. A. Klein (Secretariat for Promoting Christian Unity)
The Rev. Dr. C. H. Mau, Jr. (Lutheran World Federation)
The Rev. Dr. D. F. Martensen (Lutheran World Federation)
Prof. Dr. V. Vajta (Lutheran World Federation)

B.

DOCUMENTATION OF ORDINATION LITURGIES
(compiled by D. Frieder Schulz, Heidelberg)

SUMMARY CONTENTS

Introduction, Abbreviations, Terminology, Bibliography
Synopsis of Ordination Liturgies with Indications of Type
Main Texts from the Lutheran Ordination Liturgies
The Celebration of the Ordination of Priests According to the Roman Pontifical
Induction into the Parish Ministry in the Lutheran Churches
Induction into the Episcopal Office in the Lutheran Churches
The Celebration of the Ordination of a Bishop According to the Roman Pontifical
Literature on Ordination Liturgies

INTRODUCTION

We present a synopsis of the main Lutheran ordination liturgies and the Roman Catholic rite for the ordination of priests in order to facilitate a comparison between them and to bring out the similarities and differences. The main parts of the ten selected Lutheran formulae are then given, arranged according to type. (The letters and numbers attached to these — A 1ff., B 1ff., etc. up to F 1ff. — are also found in the synopsis, so that the reader can see the structural arrangement of the texts and, conversely, make reference to the texts as printed.) We reproduce in full the text of the Roman Catholic ordination liturgy for priests and for a bishop.

ABBREVIATIONS

C = congregation. The parts to be performed by the congregations are printed in a special type for emphasis.
a.b.c. = there is a choice of three texts.

[ ] = optional parts.
Vertical marginal lines indicate the duration of the imposition of hands or kneeling.
+ = assisting clergy share in the imposition of hands.

TERMINOLOGY

Preface = Introductory explanation of the significance of the readings.

Epiclesis = Prayer for the Holy Spirit for the ordinand, in the form of a fixed formula.

Accipe formula = Authorization formula in the imperative.

Exhortation = Exhortation in a fixed formula.

Pax = Greeting of peace, with response.

Assistants = Clergy present at and assisting in the act of ordination.

Bibliography of Liturgical Orders

(cf. Synopsis)

I   WA 38, 423ff., 432 = VII

II   Ordination, Orders of Service for Ordination and Induction, proposed by the Arnoldshain Conference, Gütersloh 1972. (Formulae agreed upon with representatives of the United Evangelical Lutheran Church of Germany [VELKD] on the basis of Luther's ordination formula.)

III   Information leaflet of the Federation of Evangelical Churches in the German Democratic Republic, 3/4 (1979), pp. 28-36. (Identical order for the churches of the Evangelical Church of the Union [EKU] in the German Democratic Republic and of the United Evangelical Lutheran Church of Germany in the German Democratic Republic, based on the Arnoldshain formula.)

IV   Proposal of the Liturgical Committee of the United Evangelical Lutheran Church of Germany, autumn 1979 (manuscript). (Draft taking the Arnoldshain formula into account.)

V   The Rite for Ordination, prepared by the Inter-Lutheran Commission on Worship, Minneapolis-Philadelphia-St. Louis 1977 (proposed revision of the 1962 formula).

VI   The celebration of the ordination of priests (according to the Roman Pontifical), International Commission on English in the Liturgy (ICEL), 1976.

VIII Den Svenska Kyrkohandboken (Swedish Church Handbook), Stockholm 1942, pp. 346-359.

IX   Suomen evankelis-luterilaisen kirkon kirkkokäsikirja III. Kirkollisten tiomitusten kirja (Church Handbook of the Evangelical Lutheran Church of Finland, III, Occasional Services Book), Helsinki 1963.

X   Agenda a Magyarországi Evangélikus Egyház lelkészei számára (*Agende* for the pastors of the Lutheran Church in Hungary), Budapest 1963.

XI   The Occasional Services from the Service Book and Hymnal, Minneapolis 1962, pp. 90-99 (Book of Order of the Lutheran churches in America).

XII   Liturgia Ndogo, 1964, Evangelical Lutheran Church in Tanzania (in Swaheli).

LC3,4
SYNOPSIS OF ORDINATION LITURGIES

	I Martin Luther Ordin. Form. 1537	**II** Arnoldshain Conf. Ordin. Form. 1972	**III** Churches in the GDR Ordin. Form. 1979
Before		Chief Liturgy as far as Collect or Creed	Chief Liturgy as far as Creed or Sermon
Word of God	Choir: Hymn invoking the Holy Spirit Collect	Presentation including reference to Confessional Obligation Ordination Address C: Hymn or Choir: Anthem [C: Creed]	Biblical Greeting C: Amen Presentation including reference to Confessional Obligation Ordination Address [Words from a member of the Cong.] C: Hymn invoking the Holy Spirit
	Two Readings Exhortation Brief Question	Introduction Three Readings A1 Long Exhortation B1 Long Question a.b. C1	Introduction Two Readings (Gospel & Epistle) A2 Long Exhortation B2 Brief Question a. C2 or long Question b.c.
Prayer	⌈ Ordinand kneels | Imposition of Hands + | Lord's Prayer ⌊ Ordination Prayer Word of Sending 1 Pet 5:2-4 Word of Blessing C: Hymn invoking the Holy Spirit	Summons to C. Ordination Prayer a.b.c. F1 Amen Commission Formula E6 ⌈ Ordinand kneels | Imposition of Hands + | Word of Sending | Words of the Assistants ⌊ Word of Blessing C: Hymn	Summons to C. ⌈ Ordinand kneels | [Imposition of Hands] + | Lord's Prayer ⌊ Ordination Prayer a.b.c. F2 C: Amen Imposition of Hands + Commission Formula E Word of Sending Words of the Assistants Word of Blessing C: Hymn
After	Continuation of the Liturgy Service with Lord's Supper	Continuation of the Liturgy Service [with Lord's Supper]	Continuation of the Liturgy Service [with Lord's Supper]

Sheet 1

IV VELKD Churches FRG Draft Agende IV 1980	V USA Lutheran Churches Draft ILCW 1977	VI Roman Catholic Church Ordination of Priests 1968
Chief Liturgy as far as Sermon	Holy Communion as far as Sermon	Mass as far as Gospel
[Biblical Greeting C: Amen] (Presentation including reference to Confessional Obligation prior to Sermon) Preamble C: Hymn invoking the Holy Spirit	C: Hymn Presentation C: Acclamation Preamble	Presentation. Recognition Endorsement C: Acclamation Ordination Address
Introduction Two Readings (Gospel & Epistle) A3 Long Question a.b. C3 or 5 Questions c. C3	Two Readings A4 Three Questions C4 with Confessional Obligation Word of Intercession C: Amen	(Three Readings—in the Liturgy of the Word) Six Questions, concluding with Promise of Obedience Word of Intercession
Summons to C. Ordinand kneels ⎤ Imposition of Hands + ⎟ Lord's Prayer ⎟ Ordination Prayer a.b.c. F3 C: Amen Word of Sending Commission Formula E8 Words of the Assistants Word of Blessing C: [Creed-] Hymn or Creed	Ordinand kneels ⎤ Imposition of Hands + ⎟ Ordination Prayer F4 C: Amen Commission Formula E9 C: Acclamation Bible and Stole with Words Sending: Acts 20:28, Pet 5:2-4 Exhortation B3 Question to C. C: Response Word of Blessing: Heb 13:20f. Pax C: Response	Ordinands kneel ⎤ Litany and Collect (with C.) ⎟ Imposition of Hands + ⎟ Silent Prayer ⎟ Prayer of Consecration with uplifted hands C: Amen C: Veni Sancte or Ps 110 with giving of Stole and Chasuble Anointing of Hands with Word Cup and Paten with Word Pax to the Ordained
Continuation of the Liturgy Service [with Lord's Supper]	Continuation of the Holy Communion	Continuation of the Mass

SYNOPSIS OF ORDINATION LITURGIES

	VII Martin Luther Ordin. Form. 1537	**VIII** Church of Sweden Prästvigning 1942	**IX** Evang. Luth. Church of Finland Prästvigning
Before		Following a Worship Service	Following a Worship Service
Sermon and Presentation	Choir: Hymn invoking the Holy Spirit Collect	In nomine Collect (kneeling) Ordination Address Prayer (kneeling) C: Amen Presentation (the Notary)	In nomine Ordination Address Prayer a.b. Presentation (the Notary)
Duties of Ministry, Commitment and Institution into Office	Two Readings Exhortation Brief Question	Introduction Readings (a choice) A5 Exhortation B4 Creed (Ordinand) Word of Intercession Five Questions C5 Vow D1 Word of Intercession Commission Formula E1 Giving of Certificate	Introduction Readings (a choice) A6 Brief Exhortation B5 Creed (Ordinand) Word of Intercession Four Questions C6 [Oath of Office] D2 Word of Intercession Commission Formula E2
Prayer, Imposition of Hands, Sending and Blessing	Ordinand kneels Imposition of Hands + Lord's Prayer Ordination Prayer Word of Sending 1 Pet 5: 2-4 Word of Blessing C: Hymn invoking the Holy Spirit	Choir: Veni Sancte with Giving of Mass Vestment Ordinand kneels Imposition of Hands + Lord's Prayer Ordination Prayer F5 Word of Sending 1 Pet 5: 2-4 Blessing C: Hymn	C: Hymn or Choir: Anthem With Giving of Mass Vestment Ordinand kneels Imposition of Hands + Lord's Prayer Ordination Prayer F6 Word of Sending 1 Pet 5: 2-4 Blessing C: Hymn
After	Continuation of the Liturgy Service with Lord's Supper	Departure	Departure

Sheet 2

X Lutheran Church in Hungary Ordin. Form.	XI USA Lutheran Churches Ordin. Form. 1962	XII ELC Tanzania NWD Ordin. Form.
Worship Service	Holy Communion as far as Prayer of the Church	Special Ordination Service
In nomine C. Amen Presentation Ordination Sermon C: Hymn or Choir: Anthem	C: Veni Sancte Presentation (the Secretary) Collect a.b. C: Amen	In nomine Ordination Sermon Prayer Presentation (the Secretary)
Introduction Four Readings (Gospel & Epistle) A7 Word of Conclusion Creed (Ordinand) Word of Intercession Five Questions C7 Handshake Oath of Office D3	Preamble and Introduction Three Readings (Gospel & Epistle) A8 Exhortation B6 C: Creed Four Questions C8 Vow D4 Word of Intercession Ordinand kneels Imposition of Hands Epiclesis E4	Introduction Readings (a choice) Exhortation B7 Creed (Ordinand) Word of Intercession Seven Questions C9 Oath of Office D5 Word of Intercession Commission Formula E5
C: Hymn invoking the Holy Spirit Ordinand kneels Imposition of Hands + Lord's Prayer Ordination Prayer F7 Commission Formula E3 Osculum pacis Word of Blessing Words of the Assistants	Accipe Formula E4 [Bible and Stole] Lord's Prayer Ordination Prayer F8 Word of Blessing	Ordinand kneels Stole, Bible, Cup with Words Imposition of Hands + Epiclesis E5 Accipe Formula E5 Giving of Certificate Ordination Prayer F9 Lord's Prayer Word of Sending 1 Pet 5:2-4 Choir: Anthem
Continuation of the Liturgy Service with Lord's Supper	Continuation of the Holy Communion	The Lord's Supper follows

Notes on the Character of the Ordination Liturgies
(cf. the synopsis with the orders I to XII)

1. It is clear from the synopsis that all the *Lutheran ordination liturgies* derive from the new simplified form drawn up by Luther. The basic core of this is the Word of God (ad hoc readings, exhortation, question) and prayer (the Lord's Prayer as basic biblical prayer and ordination prayer with invocation of the Holy Spirit, meanwhile imposition of hands together with other ministers, then the commissioning and blessing). Luther reduced the variety of traditional symbolic rites to the biblically attested imposition of hands and connected the ritual action to the preceding biblical foundational texts.

2. On this basis (I. VII) *two types of order* developed. The first type (II to V) kept closer to Luther's own formula whereas in the second type (VIII to XII) additions were made which derive from medieval ordination rites of the church. These consist for the most part of extra-Roman liturgical traditions such as *investiture* (clothing in official vestments), *porrectio instrumentorum* (Bible, chalice) with prescribed formulae, the ordinand's confession of faith, "priestly oath", *pax* and a series of questions about obligations undertaken. To some extent, these additional rites were also taken into the Anglican tradition. The incorporation of biblical readings into the ordination act is retained.

3. The revision of the *Roman Catholic rite of ordination* after the Second Vatican Council (with a return to basic forms of the ancient church) led to a manifest concentration on the core biblical passages (incorporation of the ad hoc readings into the "liturgy of the Word", prayer and imposition of hands as the core of ordination), while an interpretative function was assigned to the symbolic rites. This made it possible to include the Roman Catholic ordination rite in the synopsis and to relate it to the similar simplification in Luther's formula. At the same time the influence of the revised Roman Catholic rite on the draft revision of the American Lutherans became evident.

4. A *comparison* of the Lutheran ordination liturgies with one another and with the Roman Catholic ordination liturgy shows that the following items must be considered as the common core of an ordination liturgy: presentation, sermon, Bible readings, obligatory question, act of prayer accompanied by imposition of hands, special commissioning to service (partly accompanied by symbolic rites). The act of ordination is also in principle associated with a congregational service including the Lord's Supper, and the congregation is explicitly a partner in the act of ordination through hymns, prayers and acclamations.

5. In *Lutheran churches in the English speaking world*, the ordination liturgies were influenced by the ordinal of the Anglican tradition (XI. XII). Conversely, in the present revision of the Anglican ordination liturgy a convergent development is observable which deserves attention by the Lutheran-Catholic dialogue. Mention should be made here of: the Ordinal of the Church of South India 1958/63; the Ordinal of the Anglican-Methodist unity talks 1968; draft revision of the Episcopal Church USA 1970; Series 3 Ordination Services of the Church of England 1977 (for trial use until 1980); Common Ordinal 1977 (an attempt to find an English consensus formula). In sequence, structure and development there is a considerable correspondence to the concept of revision in V and VI.

6. In the *shaping of the ordination prayer* (which according to general Christian consensus includes the epiclesis of the Person related to the imposition of hands as the ritual core of the ordination) there is a notable recent tendency, even on practical grounds, to combine the corporate imposition of hands with a set prayer (recited from memory) and to relate it appropriately to the (mostly lengthy) ordination prayer uttered without the imposition of hands. The text spoken at the laying on of hands can precede the ordination prayer (VIII. IX. XI. XII) or follow it (II. III) or be inserted as the middle section in a threefold ordination prayer (CSI and recent Anglican revision drafts). That the intention is not to provide an alternative to an imposition of hands lasting throughout the whole act of prayer (as I. VII. III. IV) is clear from the Roman Catholic rite in which the imposition of hands (during silent prayer) precedes the prayer of consecration; this latter prayer is then offered with outstretched hands (as, so to speak, a continued imposition of hands in a different way). In the Roman Catholic rite of episcopal consecration we have, moreover, another example of a threefold prayer of consecration, with the epiclesis (its central part) spoken by the consecrating bishop together with the other bishops assisting in the consecration.

Main Texts from the Lutheran Ordination Liturgies

A. READINGS

Luther's example is followed in the arrangement of all Lutheran orders: the basic elements are the Word of God (with exhortation and question) and prayer with imposition of hands (with commissioning and blessing). The following ordination readings are found in almost all the orders: Mt 28: 18-20; Jn 20: 21-23; 2 Cor 5: 19-20; Eph 4: 11-13. With the exception of Mt 28, all these readings are also found in the choice of readings offered for the "liturgy of the Word" portion of the Catholic ordination rite.

A 1: Mt 28 : 18-20; 2 Cor 5 : 19-20; Eph 4 : 11-13.

A 2: Mt 28 : 18-20; Jn 20 : 21b-23; 1 Cor 12 : 4-11; Rom 12 : 3-6; 2 Cor 5 : 19-20; Eph 4 : 11-13; 1 Pet 4 : 10-11; Isa 52 : 7.

A 3: Mt 28 : 18-20; Jn 20 : 21-23; 2 Cor 5 : 19-20; Eph 4 : 11-13 or other suitable epistle.

A 4: Jn 20 : 21-23; Mt 28 : 18-20; 1 Tim 3 : 1-3.6-7.

A 5: Mt 28 : 18-20; Jn 21 : 15-17; Jn 20 : 21-23; Jn 15 : 4-5; Acts 20 : 28; 2 Cor 5 : 17-20; 1 Cor 4 : 1-2; 2 Cor 3 : 4-6; Jn 15 : 16; Jer 15 : 19; Mt 10 : 32-33; Mt 5 : 13-16; 2 Cor 10 : 17-18; Eph 6 : 13.

A 6: Mt 28 : 18-20; Jn 21 : 15-17; Jn 15 : 16; Jn 20 : 21–23; Acts 20 : 28; 2 Cor 5 : 18-20; 2 Tim 2 : 15; 1 Cor 4 : 1-2; Eph 4 : 11-13; 1 Tim 4 : 12-16.

A 7: Mt 28 : 18-20; Jn 20 : 21-23; 2 Cor 5 : 18-20; Eph 4 : 11-13.

A 8: Jn 20 : 21-23; Mt 28 : 18-20; 1 Tim 3 : 1-4a.6-7.

B. EXHORTATION

At the end of the Bible readings, the duties of the ministry are set forth in a longer or shorter exhortation. The longer exhortation is followed by a summarizing question; the shorter exhortation is followed by three to seven questions in which the duties of the ministry are specified. Female ordinands are addressed: Dear Sister.

B 1: Liturgy II (Arnoldshain Conference)

These words of sacred Scripture teach us the commission and promise given by our Lord to his church.

Because of their baptism, all Christians have the duty of witnessing and serving in the world. All offices in the church are meant to serve the fulfilment of this mission.

It is the duty of the congregation to provide for the public proclamation of the gospel by those who are ready and have been prepared for this task.

Dear Brother, you are now to be authorized to preach, to baptize and to administer the Lord's Supper.

In worship, instruction and pastoral care, you are to cooperate in building up the congregation and in encouraging it for its ministry in the world.

The source and the standard of this mission is the witness of Holy Scripture.

The church's confession and fraternal consultation will strengthen you in the faith we share, and help you rightly to proclaim the Word of God today.

B 2: Liturgy III (GDR)

Dear Brothers and Sisters in Christ:

By baptism you have been called to witness to and serve the gospel in the world. Every labour in the congregation of Jesus Christ serves the accomplishment of this mission. The Lord calls individuals to special ministries. You need the congregation. They need you.

Dear Brothers (Dear Sisters):

You are now being charged to proclaim the gospel publicly and to administer baptism and the Lord's Supper in accordance with the command of our Lord. You are called by preaching and teaching, instruction and pastoral care, to cooperate in the building up of the congregation, to encourage it to serve in the world, and to seek the unity of the whole Christian family.

The Holy Scriptures have been given you as the source and standard of your proclamation. In this task you will find help and guidance from the confessions of our church which contain the testimony of those who went before us.

In the words of your proclamation, the congregation is to seek and to hear the Word of its Lord, just as you yourself are to welcome the congregation's measuring of your words by the Scriptures and the help they will afford you in encouragement, counsel and reproof. Your consultation with your brothers and sisters who labour with you for the furtherance of the Word of God and your own continuing study are essential for your ministry. In this ministry you stand not alone but with all your other colleagues within the community of the whole church. You will be upheld by their prayers. Our church will support you and care for you.

Mutual confidence shall be the hallmark of our common ministry. Respect the order of our church, therefore. Cherish that which makes the gospel more accessible and be helpful in seeking new avenues for it.

In this ministry you are set within the fellowship of all your colleagues and will be upheld by the prayers of the congregation. Our church promises solemnly to support you and to care for you.

Respect the order of our church, keep inviolable the oath of secrecy in pastoral matters and so order your life that it may not belie your witness.

In all your ministry, the Lord's promise remains valid for you, even if doubt and disappointment should test you, even if sacrifice and suffering are required of you. He keeps his word and never forsakes his own.

You are solemnly enjoined to keep inviolate all confidences entrusted to you in confession and pastoral work. Help people to live thankfully and to die comforted in the faith. Give no one up for lost. Assist all who need your help.

Remember that you will have to give account to God for your ministry. Beware lest you who preach to others should yourself be found unworthy. Be constant in prayer. Remember your own need for pastoral care. The promise of the Lord is for you, too, in all your ministry, even if doubts and disappointments assail you, or if sacrifice and suffering should be laid upon you for Christ's sake. It is the Lord himself who sends you forth. He keeps his word. He leads his church to the appointed goal. He says to you: Let my grace be sufficient for you; for my strength is made perfect in weakness.

B 3: Liturgy V (USA 1977)

After the Bible and stole have been handed over with formulae and the reading of Acts 20:28 and 1 Peter 5:2-4:

Care for God's people; bear their burdens, not betraying their confidences. So discipline yourselves in life and teaching that you preserve the truth, giving no occasion for false security or illusory hope. And, be of good courage, for God himself has called you, and your labor in the Lord is not in vain.

B 4: Liturgy VIII (Sweden)

The bishop then says:

May the Lord give you grace to keep these words faithfully in your heart. They are a touchstone for your conduct and a reminder of your responsibility. May they make you more alert and kindle your zeal, sanctifying you now and always for the service of the Chief Shepherd.

The church of God looks to you to take to heart the significance of the pastoral office which is conferred on you today, and the sacred duties which it lays upon you. In faithful prayer in the Name of Jesus may you seek from God the grace and strength to prove true ministers of the Lord in both word and life.

May the Lord help you to fight the good fight of faith and to attain that everlasting life to which you are called.

B 5: Liturgy IX (Finland)

You are encouraged by these words to offer yourselves willingly at all times in the service of the Chief Shepherd. Take them as a touchstone for your life and conduct and as a reminder that you must give account before God.

B 6: Liturgy XI (USA 1962)

And now we exhort you, in the Name of our Lord Jesus Christ, that you be mindful of the holy Office to which you are called, having always in your hearts how great a treasure is committed to your charge. For the flock over which the Holy Ghost doth make you overseers is made up of the sheep of Christ, which he hath purchased with his Blood. Never cease your labor and diligence to bring those committed to your charge to the faith and knowledge of God, and to the fulness of life in Christ.

B 7: Liturgy XII (Tanzania)

May the Lord grant you grace to treasure these words in your hearts. May these same words guide your lives and remind you of your call. May each of you be adorned and enabled with purity of life in the service of the Chief Shepherd.

The church of God expects you this day to accept the pastoral ministry along with other tasks that may be given to you with an understanding of the importance of this ministry. In faith offer prayers to God in the Name of Jesus, be filled with grace and power that your words and deeds may show you to be faithful servants of the Lord's truth. May the Lord enable you to fight the good fight of faith, so that in the end you will receive the (gift of) eternal life to which you have been called.

C. QUESTIONS

The obligatory questions to be put to ordinands are of two kinds: either a single question embodying in summary form the content of the exhortation or else a set of three to seven separate questions embodying the substance of the exhortation or the summary question with which the exhortation concludes. Female ordinands are addressed: Dear Sister.

C 1: Liturgy II (Arnoldshain Conference)

Dear Brother: If you truly desire to exercise faithfully in accordance with the will of God the ministry of public proclamation into which you are now called, to preach the gospel of Jesus Christ as it has been committed to us in Holy Scripture and attested in the confession of our church (congregation), to administer the sacraments in accordance with their institution, to keep inviolate the secrets entrusted to you in confession and in the exercise of your pastoral responsibilities, and so to conduct yourself in a manner worthy of this commission, will you promise this now in the presence of God and this congregation by saying yes.

Response: Yes, with God's help.

C 2: Liturgy III, third text (GDR)

Dear Brother: Are you ready to accept the call to this ministry relying on God's grace? If so, answer: Yes, with God's help.

Response: Yes, with God's help.

C 3: Liturgy IV, first text (VELKD)

Dear Brother: What is required of us as pastors and preachers has been set forth in these words. I therefore ask you, in the presence of God and of this congregation: Are you ready to exercise the ministry committed to you faithfully and in accordance with the will of God, to proclaim the gospel of Jesus Christ as set down in Holy Scripture and attested in the confession of our Evangelical Lutheran Church, to administer the sacraments in accordance with their institution, to guard the secrecy of confession and the obligation of pastoral confidentiality, and to live in obedience to your Lord? If so, answer: Yes, with God's help.

Response: Yes, with God's help.

C 3: Liturgy IV, third text (VELKD)

Dear Brother (Dear Sister): You have heard in these words of Holy Scripture what is required of us as servants in the ministry of proclamation. I therefore put to you the following questions:

Are you ready to proclaim the gospel of Jesus Christ as set forth in the Holy Scriptures and attested to in the confession of our Evangelical Lutheran Church?

Response: I am.

Are you ready, in accordance with the orders of the church, to administer baptism and the Lord's Supper as they have been instituted by Jesus Christ, to the praise of God and for the salvation of his people?

Response: I am.

Are you ready, even if it means you must suffer in consequence, to respect the secrecy of confession and the obligation of pastoral confidentiality, and to grant absolution to all who seek it in faith?

Response: I am.

Are you ready to befriend the sick and the solitary, to assist those in distress and to plead the cause of the oppressed?

Response: I am.

Are you ready to live as a faithful disciple of your Lord Jesus Christ and to conduct yourself in every respect in such a manner that your testimony may not be placed in doubt?

Response: I am, God helping me, through Jesus Christ and by the power of the Holy Spirit. Amen.

C 4: Liturgy V (USA 1977)

P: Are you persuaded that the Lord has called you to the ministry of Word and Sacraments, and are you willing to assume this office?

R: Yes.

P: The Church in which you are to be ordained confesses that the holy Scriptures are the written Word of God and the only judge, rule, and norm of faith and life. We believe, teach and confess the Apostles', Nicene, and Athanasian creeds and acknowledge the Lutheran Confessions (— the unaltered Augsburg Confession and its Apology, the large and small catechisms of Martin Luther, the Smalcald Articles, the Treatise on the Power and Primacy of the Pope, and the Formula of Concord —) as true witnesses and faithful expositions of the holy

Scriptures. Will you therefore preach and teach in accordance with the holy Scriptures and these confessions?

R: I will.

P: Will you be diligent in your use of the means of grace? Will you pray for God's people and nourish them with his Word and holy Sacraments, leading them in faithful service and holy living?

R: Yes, with the help of God.

C 5: Liturgy VIII (Sweden)

In the presence of God and of this congregation I put to you the following questions:

Is it your desire, in the name of the Triune God, to accept the holy office of the ministry and to labour to ensure that this office is fulfilled by you in every respect to the glory of God and the salvation of souls?

The ordinands answer together: It is.

Will you proclaim God's Word purely and clearly to the best of your knowledge and conscience, as it has been given to us in the Holy Scripture and attested in the confessions of our church?

The ordinands answer together: I will.

Will you serve the congregation faithfully and willingly, urging the people to live godly lives, practising Christian pastoral care for the sick, the poor and the defenceless, and in accordance with the grace bestowed by God comforting and setting upright troubled and burdened souls?

The ordinands answer together: I will.

Will you also faithfully govern yourselves in accordance with the statutes and order of the church, exercise due obedience to those set over you and willingly comply with whatever is entrusted to you to do?

The ordinands answer together: I will.

Will you so order your life that you may become an example for all and an offence to no one?

The ordinands answer together: I will.

C 6: Liturgy IX (Finland)

In the name of the Triune God, are you willing to accept the office of pastor?
Response: I am.

Will you fulfil this ministry truly and faithfully in all respects, to the glory of God and the edification of the congregation?
Response: I will.

Will you continue always to abide in the pure Word of God and to grow in the knowledge thereof, keep yourself from all false doctrine, truly proclaim Jesus Christ and administer the holy sacraments in accordance with Christ's institution?
Response: I will.

Will you so order your life that you may become an example for the congregation and provoke no offence?
Response: I will.

C 7: Liturgy X (Hungary)

Will you now respond to the following questions in attestation of your firm resolve to enter the pastoral ministry:

Is it with sincere conviction and a good conscience that you accept the ministry of pastor in our Lutheran church?
Response: It is and I do.

Do you resolve in this ministry, faithfully to follow Jesus Christ, the Lord and head of the church, to proclaim his gospel purely and sincerely, and to administer the sacraments in accordance with Christ's institution?
Response: I do indeed.

Do you solemnly vow to serve the upbuilding of our church with dedication and loyalty and by an exemplary life?
Response: I so vow.

Do you promise to observe faithfully the constitution of our Lutheran church as legally established?
Response: I so promise.

Are you ready to confirm this decision and vow by handshake and oath?
Response: I am so ready.

C 8: Liturgy XI (USA 1962)

Are you now ready to take upon you this Holy Ministry, and faithfully to serve therein?

Each candidate shall answer in turn: Yes, by the help of God.

Will you preach and teach the Word of God in accordance with the Confessions of the Church, and will you administer the Holy Sacraments after the ordinance of Christ?

Answer: Yes, by the help of God.

Will you be diligent in the study of Holy Scripture, instant in prayer, and faithful in the use of the Means of Grace?

Answer: Yes, by the help of God.

Will you adorn the doctrine of God our Saviour by a holy life and conversation?

Answer: Yes, by the help of God.

C 9: Liturgy XII (Tanzania)

Bishop: Before God and this congregation I ask you: Do you accept the holy pastoral ministry in the name of the Triune God, will you endeavour to execute it to the glory of God and the salvation of the people?

Ordinand: Yes, I will.

Bishop: Will you rightly preach God's Word as it is contained in the Holy Scriptures, and as witnessed to by the creeds of the church? Will you minister aright the holy sacraments?

Ordinand: Yes, I will.

Bishop: Will you serve the church in faithful diligence and love, admonishing its members to remain steadfast in the faith of the Lord Jesus Christ?

Are you willing to help the poor, to visit regularly the sick and disabled and constantly in this way to bring joy to the broken-hearted and to show them the Christian way, and will you seek the lost sheep and pray for them?

Ordinand: Yes, I will.

Bishop: concerning the matter of freeing people from their sins, will you retain the confidentiality of private confession?

Ordinand: Yes, I will.

Bishop: Will you fulfil all orders of the church, and will you gladly obey your superiors in accordance with the constitution of the Evangelical Lutheran Church in Tanzania in the Northwestern diocese?

Ordinand: Yes, I will.

Bishop: Will you be diligent, upright, and a wholesome example to all people without being a stumbling-block to them, and will you nurture and care for your family? Will you be diligent in daily prayer and reading of God's Word?

Ordinand: Yes, I will.

D. OATH OF OFFICE (SOLEMN VOW)

Only in certain ordination orders do we find the oath of office as an additional public obligation, following the obligatory questions and answers. The text of the vow is read out by an assistant and repeated by the ordinand, section after section. When the ordination order does not include this legally binding vow, the practice is either for a standard form of ordination vow to be signed prior to the ordination or else for the public response to the ordination questions to be regarded as a legally binding commitment, to which reference is made in the preamble (Order II. III. IV).

D 1: Liturgy VIII (Sweden)

In the presence of the omniscient God and mindful of the great day of reckoning, I (N.N.), (X.X.) etc. promise to do all this truly and sincerely by God's grace and help.

D 2: Liturgy IX (Finland)

The notary reads the oath of office prescribed in article 96 of the church law. The ordinands then read, each in turn, the introductory and concluding portions of the oath. At the beginning of the oath they give their names. The oath of office can also be made separately in the context of the ordination.

D 3: Liturgy X (Hungary)

I (N.N.) swear by the living God Father, Son and Holy Spirit, to strive with all my strength and all my capacities to fulfil my calling as a Lutheran pastor, to proclaim the gospel of our Lord Jesus Christ purely and sincerely in accordance with the whole Bible and in the sense of our church's confessions; to administer his sacraments according to Christ's own institution; truly to care for those entrusted to my charge and to keep inviolate the confidentiality of pastoral relationships; to observe and uphold the legally established order of our church; to strive for the upbuilding of our church not only by my words but also by an exemplary life and with ministering love; to perform the whole of my ministry as pastor with sacrificial fidelity to the glory of God and to the salvation of my fellow human beings. So help me God. Amen.

D 4: Liturgy XI (USA 1962)

Before God and the Lord Jesus Christ, who shall judge the quick and the dead at his appearing, I (N.N.) do promise, with his grace and help, to fulfil these sacred obligations. Amen.

D 5: Liturgy XII (Tanzania)

I *(name of the person to be ordained)* before the all-knowing God and his congregation make my oath on what has been here addressed to me. I desire and will endeavour to accomplish all of these things the Lord being my helper. I remember the judgment day which will bring everything into the open.

E. COMMISSION FORMULA

In those ordination orders which include an official vow, the legal act whereby the pastor is installed in office is concluded by a solemn commission formula ("I commit to you the office... in the Name of the Father, etc."). Except in Order XI, no provision is made here for the imposition of hands. In more recent ordination orders from the German-speaking areas, the solemn commission formula into the pastoral office (retaining the trinitarian formula in conclusion), has been transformed into a more biblical formula ("We call and send you... in the Name of the Father, etc.") and introduced following the ordination prayer (sometimes with the prolongation of the imposition of hands which accompanies the entire act of prayer and blessing). In the Roman Catholic rite of ordination, as in the case of Luther and Order V, there is no (legally required) commission formula uttered with the imposition of hands. Female ordinands are addressed: Dear Sister.

E 1: Liturgy VIII (Sweden)

Without the imposition of hands.
By the authority which has been committed to me by the congregation in accordance with God's will, I confer upon you the priestly ministry in the Name of the Father, of the Son and of the Holy Spirit.

E 2: Liturgy IX (Finland)

Without the imposition of hands.
By the authority which has been committed to me by the congregation in accordance with God's will, I confer upon you the office of the ministry, in the Name of the Father, and of the Son and of the Holy Spirit.

E 3: Liturgy X (Hungary)

The commission formula, uttered without the imposition of hands, follows the ordination prayer.
N.N. my brother in the Lord, may the Lord Jesus, who has called you to the holy ministry of the gospel, abide with you to the end. By virtue of the command of our Lord Jesus Christ when sending forth his disciples to proclaim the gospel, I commit to you now the official preaching ministry of the church, authorizing and charging you to proclaim the Word and to administer the sacraments, and send you forth to proclaim the gospel to every creature, in the Name of the Father, and of the Son and of the Holy Spirit +. Amen.

E 4: Liturgy XI (USA 1962)

The ordinand kneels. The ordaining minister lays his hands on the head of the ordinand and says the epiclesis.
The Lord bestow upon thee the Holy Ghost for the office and work of a Minister in the Church of God, now committed unto thee by the

authority of the Church through the imposition of our hands: In the Name of the Father, and of the Son, and of the Holy Ghost.

The ordinand rises for the Accipe formula.

Take thou authority to preach the Word of God, and to minister the Holy Sacraments in the Church.

E 5: Liturgy XII (Tanzania)

By the authority granted me by this diocese and under God's commission I confer upon you the pastoral ministry in the Name of God the Father, Son and Holy Spirit. Amen.

The Ordinand kneels. Stole, Bible and cup are handed over. The ordaining minister, together with the other assisting, then lays on hands and says the epiclesis with the Accipe formula.

Lord, Holy Spirit, come upon him to receive the pastoral ministry in the church of God which is being entrusted to him by the laying on of our hands. Whosoever sins he forgives, let them be forgiven; whoever he will not forgive let their sins remain with them. Receive the authority to preach God's Word and to administer the holy sacraments in the congregation where you will be sent.

E 6: Liturgy II (Arnoldshain Conference)

Without the imposition of hands.

Dear Brother: In obedience to the commission given by the Lord to his church and trusting in his promise, we call and send you to the ministry of the public proclamation of the gospel, in the Name of the Father, and of the Son, and of the Holy Spirit. Amen.

E 7: Liturgy III (GDR)

With the imposition of hands.

Dear Brother: In the confidence that God hears our prayer and in obedience to the commission given by the Lord to his church, we send you forth into the ministry of the public preaching of the Word of God and the administration of baptism and the Lord's Supper, in the Name + of the Father, and of the Son, and of the Holy Spirit.

E 8: Liturgy IV (VELKD)

Imposition of hands is continued.

Ordaining minister: Christ says: As the Father has sent me, even so send I you. In obedience to this commission given by the Lord to his church and trusting in his promise, we call and send you to serve in the ministry of the church (to proclaim publicly the gospel of Jesus Christ and to administer the sacraments). In the Name of the Father, and of the Son, and of the Holy Spirit.

Words of blessing follow.

E 9: Liturgy V (USA 1977)

Without imposition of hands. Ordinand remains kneeling.

P: Let it be acclaimed that... *(name)* ... is ordained a minister of the Word and Sacraments in the Church of Jesus Christ.

C: Amen, Thanks be to God.

P: To *him* is committed the pastoral office with authority to preach the Word and administer the Sacraments, in the Name of the Father and of the Son and of the Holy Spirit.

C: Amen.

F. ORDINATION PRAYER

The distinctive core of all ordination prayers is the prayer for the Holy Spirit (epiclesis of the Person). In some cases the Lord's Prayer is spoken first according to Luther's example. With regard to the imposition of hands the orders follow different regulations: imposition of hands at the Lord's Prayer and the ordination prayer (Order I. V. and X); imposition of hands only at the Lord's Prayer (Order VIII. IX); imposition of hands at the Lord's Prayer, ordination prayer and concluding blessing (Order [III] IV); imposition of hands only at the concluding blessing after the prayer of ordination (Order II [III]); imposition of hands only at the silent prayer before the "prayer of consecration" (in the Roman Catholic ordination rite, with outstretched hands). For female ordinands the text is adjusted accordingly: sister, etc.

F 1: Liturgy II, first text (Arnoldshain Conference)

Beloved in the Lord, let us pray for our brother:
Almighty God our heavenly Father, thou alone dost call and send forth the ministers of thy church and givest them strength and authority for their ministry. Enlighten, we beseech thee, the heart of this brother through the Holy Spirit and guide him with thy strong hand that he may fulfil his ministry faithfully to the glory of thy holy name and to the increase of thy church.

F 2: Liturgy III, second text (GDR)

Beloved in the Lord, let us pray for our brother:
Gracious God and Father, through the preaching of the cross thou hast promised to bless all who believe the gospel. Give, we beseech thee, this brother thy Spirit for the preaching of the gospel. Strengthen him with thy strength and uphold him by thy Word in all temptation and trial. By thine aid, may thy church be equipped by his ministry for its witness in the world, to the praise and glory of thy holy name.

F 3: Liturgy IV, first text (VELKD)

Almighty God our merciful Father: we thank thee that thou hast called this our brother to serve thy church in the ministry which proclaims reconciliation. Grant him, we beseech thee, the Holy Spirit that he may truly proclaim thy Word and serve thy church with the sacraments according to thy will. Preserve him in all temptation and doubt. Grant him the courage and confidence to witness thy salvation to the world. Uphold thy church and all its ministers in thy truth, until that day when thou shalt bring in thy kingdom in all its glory, through Jesus Christ our Lord.

F 4: Liturgy V (USA 1977)

Eternal God, pour out your Holy Spirit upon this your servant... *(name)* ... whom you have called to the pastoral office. Empower his proclamation of your Word so that the Church may be gathered, renewed, and strengthened. Increase and multiply the fruits and gifts of your Spirit in his life. Endow him with wisdom to equip your people for their work of ministry, for building up the body of Christ, until we all attain to the unity of the faith and the knowledge of the Son of God. To your name be glory in the Church now and forever, through Jesus Christ, our Lord.

F 5: Liturgy VIII (Sweden)

Eternal and merciful God, loving heavenly Father. We bring before thee in prayer these our brothers who have now been ordained to serve thee in the sacred office of the ministry. Thou it is who hast commissioned them. Pour out upon them now the gifts of thy Holy Spirit and give them strength to be thy witnesses. Strenghten them that they may be bold to proclaim thy word of truth and faithfully administer thy holy sacraments.

Lord Jesus Christ, our High Priest, who didst give thine own life in the sacred and perfect sacrificial offering, help them to become thy followers. Overpower their hearts with thy love so that with willing mind they may seek the erring, take unto themselves the weak and unwearyingly seek to serve thee in thy brothers. Preserve them from despondency and confirm and strengthen their hearts with the joy of being privileged to be coworkers in thy service. Hold them firmly in thy Word and in faith, now and always, and enable them finally to achieve victory in thy name. Amen.

F 6: Liturgy IX (Finland)

Almighty and eternal God, Father of our Lord Jesus Christ. We thank thee that thou dost continue to send labourers into thy harvest. We join in prayer with and offer our intercessions on behalf of those called today by thee and consecrated to the sacred office of the ministry: grant them thy Holy Spirit, that they may become thy true witnesses and confessors. O Lord Jesus Christ, our Chief Shepherd, who dost plead for us at the throne of thy Father, in mercy hear our prayers. Be with these thy servants in their work. Let thy holy presence furnish them with humility and courage, confidence and peace. Preserve them from both pride and from despondency. Fill their hearts with love for all thy children, especially the poor and sick, the suffering and the unfortunate. Preserve them from seeking human praise and from fearing human condemnation. Help them always to be mindful that we are all unprofitable servants. But, when thou dost deem them worthy to suffer for thy name, grant them the strength so to do. And when their days of labour are done, grant that they, together with all thy faithful people, may serve and praise thee in eternity. Amen.

F 7: Liturgy X (Hungary)

Lord Jesus Christ. Who didst thyself say that the harvest is great but the labourers few, and didst therefore pray the Lord of the harvest to send forth labourers into his harvest. We beseech thee, according to this thy Word, to send this our brother into thy harvest. Pour thy Holy Spirit upon him that by his words and deeds he may bear witness of thy mercy, thy love and thy peace. For thou art indeed our Lord and Redeemer, who liveth and reigneth with the Father and the Holy Spirit for ever and ever. Amen.

F 8: Liturgy XI (USA 1962)

Most merciful God, our heavenly Father, who through thy beloved Son hast bid us pray for an increase of those who labor in the Gospel: We earnestly beseech thee to bestow thy Holy Spirit upon these thy servants, upon us, and upon all who are called to the Ministry of the Word and the Sacraments. Make us to be numbered in the company of thy true evangelists, and to continue faithful and steadfast against the world, the flesh, and the devil, that in all our words and deeds we may seek thy glory and the increase of thy kingdom; through thy Son, Jesus Christ, our Lord, who liveth and reigneth with thee and the Holy Ghost, one God, world without end. Amen.

F 9: Liturgy XII (Tanzania)

Lord God of mercies, Father in heaven, we pray for these brothers to whom the holy pastoral ministry has been entrusted. It is you who have given them this ministry. Together with the new pastors we pray for all the pastors of this diocese. Enable all of them to preach the word with joy and to administer the holy sacraments aright and diligently.

Lord Jesus Christ, our High Priest who gave your life as a perfect and holy sacrifice, lead them to copy your example. Reign in their hearts and fill them with your love as they seek the lost and bring comfort and hope to the weak.

Enable them to serve you boldly among all people. Encourage them whenever they lose courage; fill them with joy as they work together in your task. Give them tolerance in all matters. Strengthen them in your Word and in faith today and always. Amen.

Ordination of Priests*
(According to the Roman Pontifical)

OUTLINE OF THE RITE

LITURGY OF THE WORD

ORDINATION OF PRIESTS

    Calling of the Candidates
    Presentation of the Candidates
    Election by the Bishop and Consent of the People

    Homily
    Examination of the Candidates
    Promise of Obedience

    Invitation to Prayer
    Litany of the Saints
    Laying on of Hands
    Prayer of Consecration

    Investiture with Stole and Chasuble
    Anointing of Hands
    Presentation of the Gifts
    Kiss of Peace

LITURGY OF THE EUCHARIST

Ordination of Priests

The ordination of priests begins after the gospel. The bishop, wearing his miter, sits at his chair.

CALLING OF THE CANDIDATES

    The candidates are called by the deacon:

Those to be ordained priests please come forward.

    Then their names are called by the deacon. Each one answers: Present, and goes to the bishop, before whom he makes a sign of reverence.

---

* Excerpts from the English translation of *The Ordination of Deacons, Priests, and Bishops* © 1976, International Committee on English in the Liturgy, Inc. All rights reserved.

PRESENTATION OF THE CANDIDATES

When the candidates are in their places before the bishop, the priest designated by the bishop says:

Most Reverend Father, holy mother Church asks you to ordain these men, our brothers, for service as priests.

■ The Bishop asks:

Do you judge them to be worthy?

He answers:

After inquiry among the people of Christ and upon recommendation of those concerned with their training, I testify that they have been found worthy.

ELECTION BY THE BISHOP AND CONSENT OF THE PEOPLE

■ Bishop

We rely on the help of the Lord God and our Savior Jesus Christ, and we choose these men, our brothers, for priesthood in the presbyteral order.

All present say: **Thanks be to God**, or give their assent to the choice in some other way, according to local custom.

HOMILY

■ Then all sit, and the bishop addresses the people and the candidates on the duties of a priest. He may use these words:

These men, your relatives and friends, are now to be raised to the order of priests. Consider carefully the position to which they are to be promoted in the Church.

It is true that God has made his entire people a royal priesthood in Christ. But our High Priest, Jesus Christ, also chose some of his followers to carry out publicly in the Church a priestly ministry in his name on behalf of mankind. He was sent by the Father, and he in turn sent the apostles into the world; through them and their successors, the bishops, he continues his work as Teacher, Priest, and Shepherd. Priests are coworkers of the order of bishops. They are joined to the bishops in the priestly office and are called to serve God's people.

Our brothers have seriously considered this step and are now to be ordained to priesthood in the presbyteral order. They are to serve Christ the Teacher, Priest and Shepherd in his ministry which is to make his own body, the Church, grow into the people of God, a holy temple.

They are called to share in the priesthood of the bishops and to be molded into the likeness of Christ, the supreme and eternal Priest. By consecration they will be made true priests of the New Testament, to preach the Gospel, sustain God's people, and celebrate the liturgy, above all, the Lord's sacrifice.

He then addresses the candidates:

My sons, you are now to be advanced to the order of the presbyterate. You must apply your energies to the duty of teaching in the name of Christ, the chief Teacher. Share with all mankind the word of God you have received with joy. Meditate on the law of God, believe what you read, teach what you believe, and put into practice what you teach.

Let the doctrine you teach be true nourishment for the people of God. Let the example of your lives attract the followers of Christ, so that by word and action you may build up the house which is God's Church.

In the same way you must carry out your mission of sanctifying in the power of Christ. Your ministry will perfect the spiritual sacrifice of the faithful by uniting it to Christ's sacrifice, the sacrifice which is offered sacramentally through your hands. Know what you are doing and imitate the mystery you celebrate. In the memorial of the Lord's death and resurrection, make every effort to die to sin and to walk in the new life of Christ.

When you baptize, you will bring men and women into the people of God. In the sacrament of penance, you will forgive sins in the name of Christ and the Church. With holy oil you will relieve and console the sick. You will celebrate the liturgy and offer thanks and praise to God throughout the day, praying not only for the people of God but for the whole world. Remember that you are chosen from among God's people and appointed to act for them in relation to God. Do your part in the work of Christ the Priest with genuine joy and love, and attend to the concerns of Christ before your own.

Finally, conscious of sharing in the work of Christ, the Head and Shepherd of the Church, and united with the bishop and subject to him, seek to bring the faithful together into a unified family and to lead them effectively, through Christ and in the Holy Spirit, to God the Father. Always remember the example of the Good Shepherd who came not to be served but to serve, and to seek out and rescue those who were lost.

EXAMINATION OF THE CANDIDATES

■ The candidates then stand before the bishop, who questions all of them together:

My sons, before you proceed to the order of the presbyterate, declare before the people your intention to undertake this priestly office.

Are you resolved, with the help of the Holy Spirit, to discharge without fail the office of priesthood in the presbyteral order as conscientious fellow workers with the bishops in caring for the Lord's flock?

Together, all the candidates answer:

I am.

■ Bishop:

Are you resolved to celebrate the mysteries of Christ faithfully and religiously as the Church has handed them down to us for the glory of God and the sanctification of Christ's people?

Candidates:

I am.

■ Bishop:

Are you resolved to exercise the ministry of the word worthily and wisely, preaching the Gospel and explaining the Catholic faith?

Candidates:

I am.

■ Bishop:

Are you resolved to consecrate your life to God for the salvation of his people, and to unite yourself more closely every day to Christ the High Priest, who offered himself for us to the Father as a perfect sacrifice?

Candidates:

I am, with the help of God.

PROMISE OF OBEDIENCE

■ Then each one of the candidates goes to the bishop and, kneeling before him, places his joined hands between those of the bishop. If this gesture seems less suitable in some places, the conference of bishops may choose another gesture or sign.

If the bishop is the candidate's own Ordinary, he asks:

Do you promise respect and obedience to me and my successors?

Candidate:

I do.

If the bishop is not the candidate's own Ordinary, he asks:

Do you promise respect and obedience to your Ordinary?

Candidate:

I do.

■ Bishop:

May God who has begun the good work in you bring it to fulfillment.

INVITATION TO PRAYER

■ Then all stand, and the bishop, without his miter, invites the people to pray:

My dear people, let us pray that the all-powerful Father may pour out the gifts of heaven on these servants of his, whom he has chosen to be priests.

Deacon (except during the Easter season):

Let us kneel.

LITANY OF THE SAINTS

The candidates prostrate themselves and, except during the Easter season, the rest kneel at their places.

The cantors begin the litany of the saints.

Lord, have mercy	**Lord, have mercy**
Christ, have mercy	**Christ, have mercy**
Lord, have mercy	**Lord have mercy**
Holy Mary, Mother of God	**Pray for us**
Saint Michael	**Pray for us**
Holy Angels of God	**Pray for us**
Saint John the Baptist	**Pray for us**

Saint Joseph	**Pray for us**
Saint Peter and Saint Paul	**Pray for us**
Saint Andrew	**Pray for us**
Saint John	**Pray for us**
Saint Mary Magdalene	**Pray for us**
Saint Stephen	**Pray for us**
Saint Ignatius of Antioch	**Pray for us**
Saint Lawrence	**Pray for us**
Saint Perpetua and Saint Felicity	**Pray for us**
Saint Agnes	**Pray for us**
Saint Gregory	**Pray for us**
Saint Augustine	**Pray for us**
Saint Athanasius	**Pray for us**
Saint Basil	**Pray for us**
Saint Martin	**Pray for us**
Saint Benedict	**Pray for us**
Saint Francis and Saint Dominic	**Pray for us**
Saint Francis Xavier	**Pray for us**
Saint John Vianney	**Pray for us**
Saint Teresa of Avila	**Pray for us**
Saint Catherine of Siena	**Pray for us**
All holy men and women	**Pray for us**
Lord, be merciful	**Lord, save your people**
From all evil	**Lord, save your people**
From every sin	**Lord, save your people**
From everlasting death	**Lord, save your people**
By your coming as man	**Lord, save your people**
By your death and rising to new life	**Lord, save your people**
By your gift of the Holy Spirit	**Lord, save your people**
Be merciful to us sinners	**Lord, hear our prayer**
Guide and protect your holy Church	**Lord, hear our prayer**
Keep the pope and all the clergy in faithful service to your Church	**Lord, hear our prayer**
Bring all peoples together in trust and peace	**Lord, hear our prayer**
Strengthen us in your service	**Lord, hear our prayer**
Bless these chosen men	**Lord, hear our prayer**
Bless these chosen men and make them holy	**Lord, hear our prayer**
Bless these chosen men, make them holy, and consecrate them for their sacred duties	**Lord, hear our prayer**

Jesus, Son of the living God **Lord, hear our prayer**
Christ, hear us **Christ, hear us**
Lord Jesus, hear our prayer **Lord Jesus, hear our prayer**

■ The bishop alone stands and, with his hands joined, sings or says:

**Hear us, Lord our God,
and pour out upon these servants of yours
the blessing of the Holy Spirit
and the grace and power of the priesthood.
In your sight we offer these men for ordination:
support them with your unfailing love.**

We ask this through Christ our Lord.

R. Amen

Deacon:

Let us stand.

LAYING ON OF HANDS

■ Then all stand. One by one the candidates go to the bishop and kneel before him. The bishop lays his hands on the head of each, in silence.

Next all the priests present, wearing stoles, lay their hands upon each of the candidates, in silence. After the laying on of hands, the priests remain on either side of the bishop until the prayer of consecration is completed.

PRAYER OF CONSECRATION

■ The candidates kneel before the bishop. With his hands extended over them, he sings the prayer of consecration or says it aloud:

**Come to our help,
Lord, holy Father, almighty and eternal God;
you are the source of every honor and dignity,
of all progress and stability.
You watch over the growing family of man
by your gift of wisdom and your pattern of order.
When you had appointed high priests to rule your people,
you chose other men next to them in rank and dignity
to be with them and to help them in their task;
and so there grew up
the ranks of priests and the offices of levites,
established by sacred rites.**

In the desert
you extended the spirit of Moses to seventy wise men
who helped him to rule the great company of his people.
You shared among the sons of Aaron
the fullness of their father's power,
to provide worthy priests in sufficient number
for the increasing rites of sacrifice and worship.
With the same loving care
you gave companions to your Son's apostles
to help in teaching the faith:
they preached the Gospel to the whole world.

Lord,
grant also to us such fellow workers,
for we are weak and our need is greater.

Almighty Father,
grant to these servants of yours
the dignity of the priesthood.
Renew within them the Spirit of holiness.
As co-workers with the order of bishops
may they be faithful to the ministry
that they receive from you, Lord God,
and be to others a model of right conduct.

May they be faithful in working with the order of bishops,
so that the words of the Gospel may reach the ends of the earth,
and the family of nations,
made one in Christ,
may become God's one, holy people.

We ask this through our Lord Jesus Christ, your Son,
who lives and reigns with you and the Holy Spirit,
one God, for ever and ever.

R. Amen.

INVESTITURE WITH STOLE AND CHASUBLE

After the prayer of consecration, the bishop, wearing his miter, sits, and the newly ordained stand. The assisting priests return to their places, but some of them arrange the stoles of the newly ordained as they are worn by priests and vest them in chasubles.

ANOINTING OF HANDS

- Next the bishop receives a linen gremial and anoints with chrism the palms of each new priest as he kneels before him. The bishop says:

**The Father anointed our Lord Jesus Christ
through the power of the Holy Spirit.
May Jesus preserve you to sanctify the Christian people
and to offer sacrifice to God.**

While the new priests are being vested in stoles and chasubles and the bishop is anointing their hands, the hymn Veni, Creator Spiritus or the following antiphon may be sung with Psalm 110.

**Christ the Lord,
a priest for ever in the line of Melchizedek,
offered bread and wine.**

The antiphon is repeated after every two verses. Glory to the Father is not said. The psalm is interrupted and the antiphon repeated when the hands of all the priests have been anointed.

Any other appropriate song may be sung.

Then the bishop and the new priests wash their hands.

PRESENTATION OF THE GIFTS

- The deacon assists the bishop in receiving the gifts of the people and then he prepares the bread on the paten and the wine and water in the chalice for the celebration of Mass. He brings the paten and chalice to the bishop, who hands them to each of the new priests as he kneels before him. The bishop says:

Accept from the holy people of God the gifts to be offered to him. Know what you are doing, and imitate the mystery you celebrate: model your life on the mystery of the Lord's cross.

KISS OF PEACE

- Lastly, the bishop stands and gives the kiss of peace to each of the new priests, saying:

Peace be with you.

The priest responds:

And also with you.

If circumstances permit, the priests present also give the kiss of peace to the newly ordained.

Meanwhile, the following antiphon may be sung with Psalm 100.

You are my friends, says the Lord, if you do what I command you.

The antiphon is repeated after every two verses. Glory to the Father is not said. The psalm is interrupted and the antiphon repeated when all have received the kiss of peace.

Any other appropriate song may be sung, or:

**No longer do I call you servants, but my friends,
because you know all that I have done among you (alleluia).
— Receive the Holy Spirit as an Advocate among you:
it is he whom the Father will send you (alleluia).
You are my friends if you do the things I command you.
— Receive the Holy Spirit as an Advocate among you.
Glory to the Father...
— It is he whom the Father will send you (alleluia).**

Liturgy of the Eucharist

The rite for the concelebration of Mass is followed with these changes:

a) The preparation of the chalice is omitted.
b) In Eucharistic Prayer I, the special form of Father, accept this offering is said:

**Father, accept this offering
from your whole family
and from those you have chosen for the order of priests.
Protect the gifts you have given them,
and let them yield a harvest worthy of you.**

[Through Christ our Lord. Amen.]

Induction into the Parish Ministry in the Lutheran Churches

In Sweden, Finland, the USA, the Arnoldshain Conference, the German Democratic Republic and in the Federal Republic of Germany there are separate liturgical orders for this act. There is no separate Catholic rite (but cf. *Lit. Jahrbuch 22*, 1972, pp. 183ff. and 23, 1973, pp. 122ff.). In structure these orders follow the pattern of the respective ordination liturgies, while the selection of readings, and the contents of the exhortation, questions, and prayers usually have special reference to the specific ministry.

In the choice of readings we find, in addition to the passages provided for ordination, the following: Mt 28:18-20; Eph. 4:11-13; 2 Cor 5:18-20, above all Jn 21:15-17; Acts 20:28; 1 Pet 5:2-4 (cf. the word of sending in ordination); 1 Tim 4:14-16, and others.

Other distinctive features are the supplementary question put to the elders about their obligations, an exhortation to the congregation, and the handing over (or the reading aloud) of the certificate of call.

The following differences are worthy of note:

SWEDEN (cf. Ordination Formula VIII): "Installation"; absence of an introductory collect; three questions; no vow; no word of sending, but 1 Pet 5:2-4 as reading.

FINLAND (cf. Ordination Formula IX): "Installation"; two questions; no oath of office; after the prayer there is an exhortation to the congregation.

USA 1962 (cf. Ordination Formula XI): "Installation"; hymn Veni Sancte, the collect prayer and the congregational credo are omitted; one question followed by a question to the congregation, no vow; induction formula without trinitarian conclusion and without imposition of hands; Lord's Prayer said after the prayer without imposition of hands.

USA 1977 (cf. Ordination Formula V): "Installation"; presentation with handing over of the letter of call; two questions, followed by a detailed question addressed to the congregation; commission formula without imposition of hands: prayer with imposition of hands is omitted; symbolic rites (visitation to font, pulpit and altar); sending, exhortation to the congregation and the words of blessing are omitted.

GERMANY (cf. Ordination Formulae II, III, and IV): presentation with reading aloud of the letter of call; after the obligatory questions and answers, further questions to the elders; concluding exhortation to the congregation. Imposition of hands only at the words of blessing. No exhortation in II and IV; word of welcome from the elders in IV.

Induction into the Episcopal Office in the Lutheran Churches

In the cases of Sweden, Finland, Hungary, Tanzania, USA and the Federal Republic of Germany there are special liturgical orders. Like the Roman Catholic rite of episcopal consecration, these orders correspond in structure throughout to the respective ordination liturgies, while account is taken of the distinctive character of the episcopal office in the choice of Scripture passages, the exhortation, the questions, the prayer, as well as in the accompanying symbolic rites.

In addition to the Scripture passages suggested for ordination, i.e., Mt 28:18-20; Eph. 4:11-13: 2 Cor 5:18-20, the following are most frequently proposed in the texts for induction to the episcopal office: Acts 20:28; 2 Tim 2:1-3; 1 Pet 5:2-4 (cf. word of sending in the ordination liturgy); Jn 21:15-17 and other passages.

The following insignificant divergences in substance should be noted (cf. Induction into the Parish Ministry):

SWEDEN (cf. Ordination Formula VIII); "Episcopal consecration"; introductory collect missing; four questions; no oath of office; handing over of the episcopal cross, cope, episcopal staff and mitre.

FINLAND (cf. Ordination Formula IX): "Episcopal consecration"; three questions; handing over of the insignia of a bishop; presentation of the letter of call.

HUNGARY (cf. Ordination Formula X). "Installation of the bishop"; no creed is required of the episcopal candidate; two questions; handing over of the episcopal cross.

TANZANIA (cf. Ordination Formula XII); "Installation of the bishop"; four questions; no oath of office; handing over of the episcopal cross, episcopal ring and episcopal robe, during the singing of the Veni Sancte; handing over of the Bible and mitre after prayer with the imposition of hands.

USA (cf. Ordination Formula XI): "Induction of a president"; preamble with *In nomine* and collect; no collect after the presentation; no creed by the congregation; two questions, no vow; Lord's Prayer after prayer without imposition of hands.

FRG (cf. Ordination Formula IV): "Induction of a bishop"; preamble with greeting and presentation; only one question; one further question to the synod members and pastors of the district; Lord's Prayer and prayer without imposition of hands. Induction formula without trinitarian conclusion and without imposition of hands; imposition of hands at the words of blessing; handing over of the episcopal cross. Concluding exhortation to pastors and synod members.

Ordination of a Bishop*
(According to the Roman Pontifical)

OUTLINE OF THE RITE

LITURGY OF THE WORD

ORDINATION OF A BISHOP

    Hymn
    Presentation of the Bishop-elect
    Apostolic Letter
    Consent of the People

    Homily
    Examination of the Candidate

    Invitation to Prayer
    Litany of the Saints

    Laying on of Hands
    Book of the Gospels
    Prayer of Consecration

    Anointing of the Bishop's Head
    Presentation of the Book of the Gospels
    Investiture with Ring, Miter, and Patoral Staff
    Seating of the Bishop
    Kiss of Peace

LITURGY OF THE EUCHARIST

CONCLUDING RITE

Hymn of Thanksgiving and Blessing
Solemn Blessing

---

* Excerpts from the English translation of *The Ordination of Deacons, Priests, and Bishops* © 1976, International Committee on English in the Liturgy, Inc. All rights reserved.

Ordination of a Bishop

HYMN

> The ordination of a bishop begins after the gospel. While all stand, the hymn Veni, Creator Spiritus is sung, or another hymn similar to it, depending on local custom.
>
> The principal consecrator and the consecrating bishops, wearing their miters, go to the seats prepared for the ordination and sit.
>
> The bishop-elect is led by his assisting priests to the chair of the principal consecrator, before whom he makes a sign of reverence.

PRESENTATION OF THE BISHOP-ELECT

> One of the priests addresses the principal consecrator:
>
> **Most Reverend Father, the Church of N. asks you to ordain this priest, N., for service as bishop.**

> If the bishop-elect is not to be ordained as a residential bishop:
>
> **Most Reverend Father, our holy mother the Catholic Church asks you to ordain this priest, N., for service as bishop.**

APOSTOLIC LETTER

■ The principal consecrator asks him:

   Have you a mandate from the Holy See?

>   He replies:
>
>   **We have.**

■ Principal consecrator:

   Let it be read.

>   Everyone sits while the document is read.

CONSENT OF THE PEOPLE

> After the reading, all present say: **Thanks be to God,** or give their assent to the choice in some other way, according to local custom.

HOMILY

■ Then the principal consecrator, while all are sitting, briefly addresses the clergy, people, and the bishop-elect on the duties of a bishop. He may use these words:

Consider carefully the position in the Church to which our brother is about to be raised. Our Lord Jesus Christ, who was sent by the Father to redeem the human race, in turn sent twelve apostles into the world. These men were filled with the power of the Holy Spirit to preach the Gospel and gather every race and people into a single flock to be guided and governed in the way of holiness. Because this service was to continue to the end of time, the apostles selected others to help them. By the laying on of hands which confers the sacrament of orders in its fullness, the apostles passed on the gift of the Holy Spirit which they themselves had received from Christ. In that way, by a succession of bishops unbroken from one generation to the next, the powers conferred in the beginning were handed down, and the work of the Savior lives and grows in our time.

In the person of the bishop, with his priests around him, Jesus Christ, the Lord, who became High Priest for ever, is present among you. Through the ministry of the bishop, Christ himself continues to proclaim the Gospel and to confer the mysteries of faith on those who believe. Through the fatherly action of the bishop, Christ adds new members to his body. Through the bishop's wisdom and prudence, Christ guides you in your earthly pilgrimage toward eternal happiness.

Gladly and gratefully, therefore, receive our brother whom we are about to accept into the college of bishops by the laying on of hands. Respect him as a minister of Christ and a steward of the mysteries of God. He has been entrusted with the task of witnessing to the truth of the Gospel and fostering a spirit of justice and holiness. Remember the words of Christ spoken to the apostles: "Whoever listens to you listens to me; whoever rejects you rejects me, and those who reject me reject the one who sent me."

He then addresses the bishop-elect:

You, dear brother, have been chosen by the Lord. Remember that you are chosen from among men and appointed to act for men and women in relation to God. The title of bishop is one not of honor but of function, and therefore a bishop should strive to serve rather than to rule. Such is the counsel of the Master: the greater should behave as if he were the least, and the leader as if he were the one who serves. Proclaim the message whether it is welcome or unwelcome; correct error with unfailing patience and teaching. Pray and offer sacrifice for the people committed to your care and so draw every kind of grace for them from the overflowing holiness of Christ.

As a steward of the mysteries of Christ in the church entrusted to you, be a faithful overseer and guardian. Since you are chosen by the Father to rule over his family, always be mindful of the Good Shepherd, who knows his sheep and is known by them and who did not hesitate to lay down his life for them.

As a father and a brother, love all those whom God places in your care. Love the priests and deacons who share with you the ministry of Christ. Love the poor and infirm, strangers and the homeless. Encourage the faithful to work with you in your apostolic task; listen willingly to what they have to say. Never relax your concern for those who do not yet belong to the one fold of Christ; they too are commended to you in the Lord. Never forget that in the Catholic Church, made one by the bond of Christian love, you are incorporated into the college of bishops. You should therefore have a constant concern for all the churches and gladly come to the aid and support of churches in need. Attend to the whole flock in which the Holy Spirit appoints you an overseer of the Church of God — in the name of the Father, whose image you personify in the Church — and in the name of his Son, Jesus Christ, whose role of Teacher, Priest, and Shepherd you undertake — and in the name of the Holy Spirit, who gives life to the Church of Christ and supports our weakness with his strength.

EXAMINATION OF THE CANDIDATE

■ The bishop-elect then rises and stands in front of the principal consecrator, who questions him:

An age-old custom of the Fathers decrees that a bishop-elect is to be questioned before the people on his resolve to uphold the faith and to discharge his duties faithfully.

My brother, are you resolved by the grace of the Holy Spirit to discharge to the end of your life the office the apostles entrusted to us, which we now pass on to you by the laying on of hands?

The bishop-elect replies:

I am.

■ Principal consecrator:

Are you resolved to be faithful and constant in proclaiming the Gospel of Christ?

Bishop-elect:

I am.

■ Principal consecrator:

Are you resolved to maintain the deposit of faith, entire and incorrupt, as handed down by the apostles and professed by the Church everywhere and at all times?

Bishop-elect:

I am.

■ Principal consecrator:

Are you resolved to build up the Church as the body of Christ and to remain united to it within the order of bishops under the authority of the successor of the apostle Peter?

Bishop-elect:

I am.

■ Principal consecrator:

Are you resolved to be faithful in your obedience to the successor of the apostle Peter?

Bishop-elect:

I am.

■ Principal consecrator:

Are you resolved as a devoted father to sustain the people of God and to guide them in the way of salvation in cooperation with the priests and deacons who share your ministry?

Bishop-elect:

I am.

■ Principal consecrator:

Are you resolved to show kindness and compassion in the name of the Lord to the poor and to strangers and to all who are in need?

Bishop-elect:

I am.

■ Principal consecrator:

Are you resolved as a good shepherd to seek out the sheep who stray and to gather them into the fold of the Lord?

Bishop-elect:

I am.

■ Principal consecrator:

Are you resolved to pray for the people of God without ceasing, and to carry out the duties of one who has the fullness of the priesthood so as to afford no grounds for reproach?

Bishop-elect:

I am, with the help of God.

■ Principal consecrator:

May God who has begun the good work in you bring it to fulfillment.

INVITATION TO PRAYER

■ Then all stand, and the bishop, without his miter, invites the people to pray:

My dear people, let us pray that almighty God in his goodness will pour out his grace upon this man whom he has chosen to provide for the needs of the Church.

Deacon (except during the Easter season):

Let us kneel.

LITANY OF THE SAINTS

The bishop-elect prostrates himself and, except during the Easter season, the rest kneel at their places.

The cantors begin the litany of saints.

Lord, have mercy	**Lord, have mercy**
Christ, have mercy	**Christ, have mercy**
Lord, have mercy	**Lord have mercy**
Holy Mary, Mother of God	**Pray for us**
Saint Michael	**Pray for us**
Holy Angels of God	**Pray for us**
Saint John the Baptist	**Pray for us**
Saint Joseph	**Pray for us**
Saint Peter and Saint Paul	**Pray for us**
Saint Andrew	**Pray for us**

Saint John	**Pray for us**
Saint Mary Magdalene	**Pray for us**
Saint Stephen	**Pray for us**
Saint Ignatius of Antioch	**Pray for us**
Saint Lawrence	**Pray for us**
Saint Perpetua and Saint Felicity	**Pray for us**
Saint Agnes	**Pray for us**
Saint Gregory	**Pray for us**
Saint Augustine	**Pray for us**
Saint Athanasius	**Pray for us**
Saint Basil	**Pray for us**
Saint Martin	**Pray for us**
Saint Benedict	**Pray for us**
Saint Francis and Saint Dominic	**Pray for us**
Saint Francis Xavier	**Pray for us**
Saint John Vianney	**Pray for us**
Saint Teresa of Avila	**Pray for us**
Saint Catherine of Siena	**Pray for us**
All holy men and women	**Pray for us**
Lord, be merciful	**Lord, save your people**
From all evil	**Lord, save your people**
From every sin	**Lord, save your people**
From everlasting death	**Lord, save your people**
By your coming as man	**Lord, save your people**
By your death and rising to new life	**Lord, save your people**
By your gift of the Holy Spirit	**Lord, save your people**
Be merciful to us sinners	**Lord, hear our prayer**
Guide and protect your holy Church	**Lord, hear our prayer**
Keep the pope and all the clergy in faithful service to your Church	**Lord, hear our prayer**
Bring all peoples together in trust and peace	**Lord, hear our prayer**
Strengthen us in your service	**Lord, hear our prayer**
Bless this chosen man	**Lord, hear our prayer**
Bless this chosen man and make him holy	**Lord, hear our prayer**
Bless this chosen man, make him holy, and consecrate him for his sacred duties	**Lord, hear our prayer**
Jesus, Son of the living God	**Lord, hear our prayer**
Christ, hear us	**Christ, hear us**
Lord Jesus, hear our prayer	**Lord Jesus, hear our prayer**

■ After the litany, the principal consecrator alone stands and, with hands joined, sings or says:

**Lord,
be moved by our prayers.
Anoint your servant with the fullness of priestly grace,
and bless him with spiritual power in all its richness.
We ask this through Christ our Lord.**

R. Amen.

Deacon:

Let us stand.

LAYING ON OF HANDS

■ All rise. The principal consecrator and the consecrating bishops stand at their places, facing the people. The bishop-elect rises, goes to the principal consecrator, and kneels before him.

The principal consecrator lays his hands upon the head of the bishop-elect, in silence. After him, all the other bishops present do the same.

BOOK OF THE GOSPEL

■ Then the principal consecrator places the open Book of the Gospels upon the head of the bishop-elect; two deacons, standing at either side of the bishop-elect, hold the Book of the Gospels above his head until the prayer of consecration is completed.

PRAYER OF CONSECRATION

■ Next the principal consecrator, with his hands extended over the bishop-elect, sings the prayer of consecration or says it aloud:

**God the Father of our Lord Jesus Christ,
Father of mercies and God of all consolation,
you dwell in heaven,
yet look with compassion on all that is humble.
You know all things before they come to be;
by your gracious word
you have established the plan of your Church.**

**From the beginning
you chose the descendants of Abraham to be your holy nation.**

**You established rulers and priests,
and did not leave your sanctuary without ministers to serve you.
From the creation of the world
you have been pleased to be glorified
by those whom you have chosen.**

The following part of the prayer is recited by all the consecrating bishops, with hands joined:

**So now pour out upon this chosen one
that power which is from you,
the governing Spirit
whom you gave to your beloved Son, Jesus Christ,
the Spirit given by him to the holy apostles,
who founded the Church in every place to be your temple
for the unceasing glory and praise of your name.**

Then the principal consecrator continues alone:

**Father, you know all hearts.
You have chosen your servant for the office of bishop.
May he be a shepherd to your holy flock,
and a high priest blameless in your sight,
ministering to you night and day;
may he always gain the blessing of your favor
and offer the gifts of your holy Church.
Through the Spirit who gives the grace of high priesthood
grant him the power
to forgive sins as you have commanded,
to assign ministries as you have decreed,
and to loose every bond by the authority which you gave to
your apostles.**

**May he be pleasing to you by his gentleness and purity of heart,
presenting a fragrant offering to you,
through Jesus Christ, your Son,
through whom glory and power and honor are yours
with the Holy Spirit
in your holy Church,
now and for ever.**

R. Amen.

After the prayer of consecration, the deacons remove the Book of the Gospels which they have been holding above the head of the new bishop. One of them holds the book until it is given to the bishop. The principal consecrator and the consecrating bishops, wearing their miters, sit.

ANOINTING OF THE BISHOP'S HEAD

■ The principal consecrator puts on a linen gremial, takes the chrism, and anoints the head of the bishop, who kneels before him. He says:

God has brought you to share the high priesthood of Christ. May he pour out on you the oil of mystical anointing and enrich you with spiritual blessings.

The principal consecrator washes his hands.

PRESENTATION OF THE BOOK OF THE GOSPELS

■ He then hands the Book of the Gospels to the newly ordained bishop, saying:

Receive the Gospel and preach the word of God with unfailing patience and sound teaching.

Afterward the deacon takes the Book of the Gospels and returns it to its place.

INVESTITURE WITH RING, MITER, AND PASTORAL STAFF

■ The principal consecrator places the ring on the ring finger of the new bishop's right hand, saying:

Take this ring, the seal of your fidelity.
With faith and love protect the bride of God, his holy Church.

Then the principal consecrator places the miter on the head of the new bishop, in silence.

Lastly, he gives the pastoral staff to the bishop, and says:

Take this staff as a sign of your pastoral office:
keep watch over the whole flock
in which the Holy Spirit has appointed you
to shepherd the Church of God.

SEATING OF THE BISHOP

■ All stand. If the ordination takes place at the bishop's chair and if the new bishop is in his own church, the principal consecrator invites him to occupy the chair; in that case the principal consecrator sits at the right of the newly ordained bishop. If the new bishop is not in his own church, he is invited by the principal consecrator to take the first place among the concelebrating bishops.

If the ordination does not take place at the bishop's chair, the principal consecrator leads the newly ordained bishop to the chair or to a place prepared for him, and the consecrating bishops follow them.

KISS OF PEACE

■ The newly ordained then sets aside his staff and receives the kiss of peace from the principal consecrator and all the other bishops.

After the presentation of the staff, and until the end of the ordination rite, the following antiphon may be sung with Psalm 96.

Alleluia, go and teach all people my Gospel, alleluia.

The antiphon is repeated after every two verses. Glory to the Father is not said. The psalm is interrupted and the antiphon repeated when all have given the kiss of peace to the new bishop.

Any other appropriate song may be sung.

Liturgy of the Eucharist

The rite for the concelebration of Mass is followed with this change:

In Eucharistic Prayer I, the special form of Father, accept this offering is said:

**Father, accept this offering
from your whole family
and from the one you have chosen for the order of bishops.
Protect the gifts you have given him,
and let him yield a harvest worthy of you.**

[Through Christ our Lord. Amen.]

Concluding Rite

HYMN OF THANKSGIVING AND BLESSING

■ At the conclusion of the prayer after communion, the hymn Te Deum is sung, or another hymn similar to it, depending on local custom. Meanwhile, the newly ordained bishop is led by the consecrating bishops through the church, and he blesses the congregation.

After the hymn, the new bishop may stand at the altar or at the chair with staff and miter and address the people briefly.

SOLEMN BLESSING

■ The following blessing may be used in place of the usual blessing. If the newly ordained bishop is the celebrant, he says:

**Lord God,
you care for your people with kindness,
you rule them with love.
Give your Spirit of wisdom
to the bishops you have made teachers and pastors.
By advancing in holiness
may the flock become the eternal joy of the shepherds.**

R. Amen.

**Lord God,
by your power you allot us
the number of our days and the measure of our years.
Look favorably upon the service we perform for you,
and give true, lasting peace in our time.**

R. Amen.

**Lord God,
now that you have raised me to the order of bishops,
may I please you in the performance of my office.
Unite the hearts of people and bishop,
so that the shepherd may not be without the support of his flock,
or the flock without the loving concern of its shepherd.**

R. Amen.

**May almighty God bless you,
the Father, and the Son, † and the Holy Spirit.**

R. Amen.

■ If the principal consecrator presides over the eucharistic liturgy, he says:

**May the Lord bless and keep you.
He chose to make you a bishop for his people:
may you know happiness in this present life
and share unending joy.**

R. Amen.

The Lord has gathered his people and clergy in unity.
By his care and your stewardship
may they be governed happily for many years.

R. Amen.

May they be obedient to God's law,
free from hardships,
rich in every blessing,
and loyally assist you in your ministry.
May they be blessed with peace and calm in this life
and come to share with you
the fellowship of the citizens of heaven.

R. Amen

May almighty God bless you,
the Father, and the Son, † and the Holy Spirit.

R. Amen.

Literature on Ordination Liturgies

ROMAN CATHOLIC CHURCH

Cooke, Bernard, *Ministry to Word and Sacraments*, Philadelphia, 1976.

Fischer, Balthasar, "Das Gebet der Kirche als Wesenselement des Weihesakraments", *Lit. Jahrbuch*, Vol. 20, 1970, pp. 166ff.

Kleinheyer, Bruno, "Überlegungen zu einer Reform des Priesterweiheritus", *Lit. Jahrbuch*, Vol. 14, 1964, pp. 202ff.

Kleinheyer, Bruno, "Weiheliturgie in neuer Gestalt", *Lit. Jahrbuch*, Vol. 18, 1968, pp. 210ff.

Lengeling, Emil, "Die Theologie des Weihesakraments nach den Zeugnissen des neuen Ritus", *Lit. Jahrbuch*, Vol. 19, 1969, pp. 142ff.

Reifenberg, Hermann, "Amtseinführung eines neuen Pfarrers, Grundgedanken und Modelle zur Neuordnung der Installation", *Lit. Jahrbuch*, Vol. 22, 1972, pp. 183ff.

CHURCHES OF THE REFORMATION
(German language region)

Brand, Eugene L., "Kirche als Familie", *Reihe Gottesdienst Heft 6*, 1976, pp. 15ff.

Brunner, Peter, "Ein Vorschlag für die Ordination in Kirchen lutherischen Bekenntnisses", *Theol. Literaturzeitung*, 100 Jg., 1975, pp. 174ff.

Schulz, Frieder, "Evangelische Ordination: Zur Reform der liturgischen Ordnungen", *Jahrbuch für Liturgik und Hymnologie*, Vol. 17, 1972, pp. 1ff.

Schulz, Frieder, "Die Ordination als Gemeindegottesdienst", *Jahrbuch für Liturgik und Hymnologie*, Vol. 23, 1979, pp. 1ff.

CHURCHES OF THE REFORMATION
(English language region)

Ordination Rites, Past and Present, ed. by W. Vos and G. Wainwright, Rotterdam, 1980.

Quere, Ralph W., "Imparting or Imploring the Spirit in Ordination Rites?", *Lutheran Quarterly* 27, 1975, pp. 322-346.

Sansom, M., *Liturgy for Ordination*, The Series 3 Services, Grove Booklet on Ministry and Worship, No. 60, Bramcote Notts. 1978.

Toon, Peter, *The Ordinal and Its Revision*, Grove Booklet on Ministry and Worship, No. 29, Bramcote Notts. 1974.

CHURCHES OF THE REFORMATION
(French language region)

"L'ordination juive à la veille du Christianisme", *La Maison-Dieu*, Paris, 138 (1979 II), pp. 7-141.

"Prières récentes d'ordination dans quelques églises chrétiennes", *La Maison-Dieu*, Paris, 139 (1979 III), pp. 73-99.

"Les réformes récentes des rites d'ordination dans les églises", *La Maison-Dieu*, Paris, 139 (1979 III), pp. 7-72.

ECUMENICAL ASPECT

Ordination und kirchliches Amt. Publication of the ecumenical working group of Protestant and Catholic theologians, Paderborn/Bielefeld, 1976, with contributions from Peter Bläser, Karl Lehmann, Peter Brunner, Hermann Kunst, Bernhard Lohse.

Ordination heute. Kirche zwischen Planen und Hoffen. Heft 5, Kassel, 1972, with contributions from Hans Dombois, Karl Lehmann, Alexander Völker.

Ratcliff, E. C., "The Ordinal of the Church of South India", *Theology* 63, 475 (January 1960), pp. 7-15.

Porter, H. B., *The Ordination Prayers of the Ancient Western Churches*, Alcuin Club Collections 49, London, 1967.

C.
SUPPLEMENTARY STUDIES

1.

Admission of Women to the Ministry
by Hervé Legrand OP and John Vikström

1. In respect of the ordination of women to the ministry, the unbroken tradition of centuries has been maintained down to the present day in our churches. Under the influence of new cultural and social factors, however, and as a result of the development of exegetical and theological methods, a variety of approaches to the question has emerged in the Lutheran churches. Similar questions have been raised within the Roman Catholic Church and have made it necessary for it to reaffirm its position in recent years (*Inter Insigniores*, 1976. For further details, see below Nos. 4ff.).

2. Neither the interruption of the earlier discipline nor its reaffirmation implies that the theological discussion has been completely resolved. In the present stage of our dialogue on the ministry it is important to bear this in mind. Hence the publication of this document.

I. THE POSITION OF THE LUTHERAN CHURCHES AND THE ROMAN CATHOLIC CHURCH

3. No uniform attitude among Lutherans:

In respect of the ordination of women, the Lutheran churches have no uniform approach. While most of the member churches of the Lutheran World Federation are in favour, a few of them are still opposed. Where the ordination of women has been introduced, it has been from the viewpoint that Holy Scripture interpreted in the light of the Confessions, not only does not prevent but even authorizes this reform. For it not only helps to enhance the churches' ministry in new social and cultural conditions but also responds to the demand for justice expected of the churches in this matter.

Where the ordination of women has been opposed, appeal has been made in the first place to biblical examples and prescriptions. These have been considered valid for all periods of time. The ordination of women has been justified by some through an appeal to the equality of man and woman, which is valid in the question of salvation. Those opposed to the ordination of women have vindicated their position by an appeal to the difference between man and woman as created by God.

It is also sometimes the case that when a Lutheran church ordains women — as e.g. in Sweden since 1958 — it inserts a conscience clause both for the bishops, who are not obliged to ordain women, and for pastors, who are not obliged to cooperate with women colleagues in liturgical and other matters, even though such an attitude can imperil the unity of the ministry and the credibility and influence of the church's evangelical witness. The force of such a conscience clause can weaken with the passage of time because of developments in experience and practice, but it is in itself a proof that there is no desire to challenge in a radical way the Christian justification for diverging views.[1]

In various ways the question of the ordination of women thus continues to provoke a theological disciplinary debate which the member churches of the Lutheran World Federation must pursue both domestically and ecumenically.[2]

4. In the Roman Catholic Church there is a clear refusal to ordain women but no solemn and binding doctrinal pronouncement on this question.

The first official document of the Roman Catholic Church to deal explicitly with the ordination of women was published by the Congre-

---

[1] For the wording of the conscience clause in Sweden see Martin Lindström, *Bibeln och bekännelsen om kvinnliga präster*, Stockholm, 1978, p. 18. It is cited from the minutes of the 1953 church synod when the ordination of women was introduced. — "Rules for cooperation within the Church of Sweden between those holding different views in the question of the admission of women to the holy ministry" were drafted on 1 December 1978 by a committee presided over by the Archbishop of Uppsala. Discussion in the Church of Sweden today centres on the question as to how, within one and the same church subject to one and the same confession, a harmonious life is spiritually and practically possible when different conscientious views are held on the question of ordination.

[2] Martin Lindström's book (see note 1), while only summarizing the debates in the Church of Sweden, is, as information however, typical for the Lutheran churches on the whole. — The Sixth Assembly of the Lutheran World Federation urged that the problem be studied in the member churches *(In Christ — A New Community, The Proceedings of the Sixth Assembly of the Lutheran World Federation*, Dar-es-Salaam, 1977, LWF Geneva, 1977, p. 206).

gation for the Doctrine of the Faith in the year 1976.[3] The key passage reads: "The Church, in fidelity to the example of the Lord, does not consider herself authorized to admit women to priestly ordination. The Sacred Congregation deems it opportune at the present juncture to explain this position of the Church."[4]

Following the customary criteria for interpreting official doctrinal statements, the following three points need to be examined in order to understand this 1976 statement correctly: (a) We are reminded of a norm, (b) we are provided with explanations differing in importance in order to justify this norm, and (c) finally considering the doctrinal statement in itself, we have to make precise the degree to which it is binding.

5. A. The Norm

The purpose of the statement is to remind people of the norm and, in the second place, it considers it "useful in the present situation to explain the doctrinal foundations". While norm and doctrine have been considered separately, they are nevertheless connected.

6. B. The Doctrinal Foundations of the Norm

In support of the norm appeal is made to doctrinal foundations which are of unequal authority and therefore clearly differ.

(i) In support of the doctrinal authority of the norm, the Sacred Congregation adduces first of all the following points:

"The Catholic Church has never felt that priestly or episcopal ordination can be validly conferred on women." This fact reflects a tradition which has remained firm in the course of the centuries and "been faithfully safeguarded by the Churches of the East" as well as the West. "Adaptation to civilizations and times" is not ruled out even in the sacramental sphere, but "in the final analysis it is the Church, through the voice of her Magisterium, that, in these various domains, decides what can change and what must remain immutable". In the present case "this practice of the Church therefore has a normative character... This norm,

---

[3] Quite apart from the classic canon 968, para. 1 "*sacram ordinationem valide recipit solus vir baptizatus*", Paul VI also declared his opposition to the ordination of women on several occasions, e.g. in his letter to Cardinal B. Alfrink, AAS 62,1970, 67; in the elevation of Catherine of Siena and Theresa of Avila to the status of church doctors, AAS 62, 1970, 593; and in two letters to Dr. Coggan, Archbishop of Canterbury, AAS 68, 1976, 599–601.

[4] *Inter Insigniores*, AAS 69, 1977, 100. English version: Declaration on the Question of the Admission of Women to the Ministerial Priesthood, Vatican Polyglot Press, Vatican City, 1976, p. 5; quoted: Declaration.

based on Christ's example, has been and is still observed because it is considered to conform to God's plan for his Church."[5]

It should also be noted that the example of Christ, according to the declaration, does not "make the matter immediately obvious" and that "to reach the ultimate meaning of Scripture, a purely historical exegesis of the texts cannot suffice".[6]

The magisterium's recognition of this "example" as a doctrinal norm, therefore, is based less on Scripture than on tradition. It is only this one point that it covers with its own authority.

7. (ii) A second stage, which does not commit the magisterium,[7] introduces the arguments based on the analogy of faith; for example, the most important of them, namely, the argument that the priest acts, especially in the celebration of the eucharist, *in persona Christi capitis*. This makes it clear that the magisterium did not want to commit itself to arguments of a symbolic sort.

8. C. The Doctrinal Authority of this Statement

Inter Insigniores is not a papal declaration. Although a declaration of the Pope can in very rare and carefully defined cases be irreformable, this does not apply to the declaration *Inter Insigniores* which was published by a Roman Congregation. Such statements can be endorsed by the Pope, either *in forma specifica*, and therefore with considerable authority, or *in forma communi*, i.e., with a lesser degree of authority. In the case of the present document, it is the latter form of endorsement.

9. The inference here is that the Roman declaration *Inter Insigniores* is characterized by its doctrinal caution. It pronounces exclusively on the subject of a centuries-old universal custom of ordaining men only, a custom which is held to be the will of Christ. Even though it has vested this statement with only minimal formal authority, this doctrinal statement will, in all probability, not be revised in the foreseeable future.

II. THE MOST IMPORTANT THEOLOGICAL REFERENCES FOR DEALING WITH THIS ISSUE (SCRIPTURE, TRADITION, SYMBOLISM)

10. Although theological reflection on the ordination of women is at different stages in the individual churches,[8] there are three traditional

---

[5] AAS 69, 108; Declaration, pp. 5, 6, 11.

[6] AAS 69, 103; Declaration, p. 7.

[7] Clarification of the official commentary in the appendix; Documentation Catholique 59, 1977, 171.

[8] Reference may be made here to *Ordination of Women in Ecumenical Perspective*, Faith and Order Paper 105, Geneva, 1980.

authorities to which reference is made: (A) Scripture, (B) Tradition and (C) the symbolic representation of Christ in his ministers.

11. A. Appeal to Scripture

To ask the New Testament about the ordination of women is to put a question to it which in this form it did not itself ask. In particular, the specific question of presidency at the eucharist was not discussed as such in the New Testament. The relation between Christ and the church, which is described in the Corpus Paulinum as analogous to marriage, was not transferred to the relationship between ministers and the church.

For their contribution to our problem, therefore, biblical scholars refer to: (i) the attitude of Jesus toward women and (ii) Pauline teaching. In doing so, they have (iii) been compelled to point out the limits imposed on the appeal to scientific exegesis.

12. (i) Jesus attitude toward women and their ministry:

The attitude adopted by Jesus to women was so new that he shocked the disciples:

— By proclaiming their equal status within marriage, he lifted women to the status of partners with the men (Mt 19:1-19; Mk 10:1-9). For Jesus, a woman is in the fullest sense a human being whatever her situation may be (he appeals to Genesis 1), and especially when she is despised: cf. the incidents of the Samaritan woman, the great sinner, the woman with an issue of blood (a ritual impurity) and the woman who anointed his head with oil.

— In his preaching ministry he allowed women to follow him and to share his ministry (Lk 8:1-3; Mk 15:40-41; Mt 27:55-56). More remarkable still is his choice of women as the first witnesses of his resurrection. The four gospels are agreed on this point as also on the commissioning of the women to announce the Good News to the brethren, i.e., to the whole church (Lk 24:5-10; Mk 16:1-8; Mt 28:5-10; Jn 20:1; 11-18).

— Yet Jesus did not choose any woman to be a member of the Twelve. Does this show his intention to exclude them from the ordained ministry which was later to develop in the church? The only purposes which can be established historically are those which are included in the symbolic act of the constitution of the Twelve. Here the vital question for Jesus was not the place which women should have in the ministry, but the announcement which he makes to the whole people (he comes to gather together all Israel, i.e., the twelve tribes) that all are judged by his word (whereby the Twelve — like the sons of Jacob — will be the eschatological judges, Mt 19:28). The symbolic significance of this action would have been nullified had Jesus included a woman or even a Samaritan.

It is wise, however, to follow certain exegetes in noting that the editorial tradition of Luke probably establishes a connection between the institution of the eucharist and the office of church leadership, i.e., the Twelve. It is underlined even more strongly that the primitive Church saw the Twelve as the custodians of the commission received from Jesus.

In short, Jesus regards men and women as full partners, both in human affairs and in the matter of salvation. He permits women to share — at least partly — in his ministry, but in a new way. Above all, he makes women the first witnesses of his resurrection. Against this background, is access to the ministries of the church open to them? The answer to this question cannot be given on the basis of exegesis alone.

13. (ii) The Pauline evidence:

The Corpus Paulinum contains three statements about the position of women in the assemblies for worship. Our reference is to the most current interpretation of these passages. One of these three passages unambiguously excludes women from presidency in the church and in the assembly; the other two passages probably imply this exclusion.

14. 1 Cor 11:3-16.

By prescribing that women can only pray aloud or make prophetic speeches in the assembly on condition that they cover their heads, Paul incidentally teaches that the man is the head of the woman. This statement, connected with Eph 5:18-33, reveals that the mutual dependence of man and woman remains at least asymmetrical. Apparently the order of creation is not set aside by the order of redemption. It is probable, therefore, that Paul would have considered the case where women presided at an assembly of both men and women as a disorder.

15. 1 Cor 14:34-35.

According to this text, women should not speak in the assemblies — in the ordinary sense of the word "speak". If something is obscure to them, all they need to do is to ask their husband about it when they get home, in order not to interrupt the speaker or even to disturb in any way. To do so would be unseemly and violate the subordination to which they are subject according to the law.[9] Many Catholic and Protestant scholars consider this passage to be an insertion.

---

[9] R. Gryson, *The Ministry of Women in the Early Church*, Collegeville, MN, 1976, p. 6.

Their grounds for doing so must be treated seriously.[10] But this hypothesis is not inescapable. Paul, without contradicting himself, is here possibly recognizing that women with the necessary charisma are equipped to prophesy in the church, especially if we interpret the word *lalein* — used here without suffix — in the way that has already been suggested. The condition for doing this is that they veil themselves and do not get involved in public discussion, and that they ask others, their own husbands especially, to explain to them the meaning of the message they have heard.[11] The argument being used here is not the order of creation but the order of appropriateness, i.e., an ethical order.[12] The authentic Pauline text, therefore, might not prohibit all women from speaking publicly in the church.

---

[10] Five arguments are usually adduced: (1) The passage appears to contradict 1 Cor 11:2-16 where it is said that women have the right to speak in Christian assemblies; (2) these verses disturb the normal argument of the chapter: if they are omitted from this passage, the text reads better; (3) in a number of versions this is shown by the transcription, for the Codex Claromontanus (D) and certain western manuscripts (Vetus Latina) and authors such as Ambrosiaster place these verses after 14:40, though this in itself is hardly evidence of interpolation; (4) certain linguistic peculiarities, such as the use of the words "permit" and "submissiveness", which are found in 1 Tim 2:11f., show, like the final argument, (5) that the development of thought in this section originates closely in the deutero-Pauline 1 Tim 2:11-12. Among the scholars who assume an interpolation here are: C. K. Barrett, *A Commentary on the First Epistle to the Corinthians*, New York-Evanston, 1968, pp. 330-333; H. Conzelmann, *1 Corinthians: A Commentary on the First Epistle to the Corinthians*, Fortress Press, Philadelphia, 1975, p. 246; he appeals to J. Weiss, J. Leipoldt, G. Fitzer. Finally, the NT scholar G. Dautzenberg, has made a detailed study of prophecy in the 1st Epistle to the Corinthians and declares in favour of an interpolation: G. Dautzenberg, *Urchristliche Prophetie, Ihre Erforschung, ihre Voraussetzung im Judentum and ihre Struktur im ersten Korintherbrief*, Stuttgart, 1975, pp. 257-263, 270-273, 290-298. His view is repeated without modification in "Botschaft und Bedeutung der urchristlichen Prophetie nach dem ersten Korintherbrief (2:6-16, 12-14)", J. Panagopoulos (ed.), *Prophetic Vocation in the New Testament and Today*, Leiden, 1977, p. 135, 10; p. 159, 81. Catholic scholars taking the same line are: J. Murphy-O'Connor, "The Non-Pauline Character of 1 Corinthians 11:2-16", *Journal of Biblical Literature* 95, 1976, p. 615; R. Gryson, *The Ministry of Women in the Early Church*, op. cit., pp. 6f.

[11] J. Héring, *The First Epistle of Saint Paul to the Corinthians*, Epworth Press, London, 1962, pp. 154f.; W. A. Meeks, "The Image of the Androgyne: Some Uses of a Symbol in Earliest Christianity", *History of Religions* 13, 1973-74, pp. 165-208, especially pp. 197-207; R. J. Kallis, "The Role of Women According to Jesus and the Early Church", C. Stuhlmüller (ed.), *Women and Priesthood. Future Directions*, Collegeville, MN, 1978, p. 53. Cf. also *Bybelsyn och bibelbruk*, Lund, 1970, pp. 118f.

[12] Cf. also W. Schrage, *Die konkreten Einzelgebote in der paulinischen Paränese. Ein Beitrag zur neutestamentlichen Ethik*, Gütersloh, 1961, p. 217.

16. 1 Tim 2:11-14.

With its categorical form, this text tips the balance in favour of the exclusion of women from the presbyterate and episcopate: "I permit no woman to teach or to have authority over man." The motive is not the example of the Lord. It is clearly stated: "For Adam was formed first, then Eve; and Adam was not deceived, but the woman was deceived and became a transgressor."

17. The exclusion of women from the teaching office and leadership, whether directly Pauline or not, is a datum of the canonical Scriptures. But scholars are not agreed whether this regulation applies to the sphere of ethics or to that of church order. If the first assertion in the Corpus Paulinum seems to be the social subordination of women to men and the first concern consists in transcending precisely this subordination by the novelty of the *in Christo* (Eph), then this ethical reality can find different forms of expression corresponding to different cultural and social environments. Other scholars note that social appropriateness is rooted in a more fundamental order. If in the Christian assembly women must be subordinate to men, the reason for this is because the sequence — God-Christ-man-woman — has its own intrinsic validity. It is therefore normal that we should rediscover this state of affairs in the reality of the ministries, even though according to Galatians 3:28 these display an eschatological character.[13]

Are we dealing with an ethical order or with a constitutional order for the church? This is a question which scientific scholarship alone cannot answer in any satisfactory way.

18. (iii) The limits imposed on the appeal to exegesis:

As has already been pointed out, exegesis alone can give no satisfactory answer to a question so concrete and so new as that of the ordination of women. This has become particularly clear in the discussion of women's ordination within the Lutheran churches. Both supporters and opponents have appealed to Holy Scripture, and representatives of the same view of the Bible have come to diametrically opposite conclusions. This is the experience on the Lutheran side. On the Catholic side, *Inter Insigniores* contains the clear recognition: "To reach the... ultimate meaning of Scripture, a purely historical exegesis of the texts cannot suffice." This assertion is explained as follows in the Congregation's semi-official

---

[13] There is perhaps no complete consistency in the Corpus Paulinum. Another reference to this would be the mention of a woman as a noted apostle in Roman 16:7; the Greek fathers were well aware that this was the case of a woman — see e.g. John Chrysostom, In Epist. ad Rom. Hom. 31, 2 (PG 60, 669).

commentary: "We must not expect the New Testament on *its own* to resolve in a clear fashion the question of the possibility of women acceding to the priesthood."[14]

19. B. The Appeal to the Tradition

(i) The continuity of the unwritten law among the Catholics:

Throughout its history "the Catholic Church has never felt that priestly or episcopal ordination can be validly conferred on women".[15] In their day the church fathers regarded such an innovation "as unacceptable in the Church. It is true that in the writings of the Fathers one will find the undeniable influence of prejudices unfavourable to women."[16] "The same conviction animates mediaeval theology, even if the Scholastic doctors, in their desire to clarify by reason the data of faith, often present arguments on this point that modern thought would have difficulty in admitting or would even rightly reject. Since that period and up to our own time, it can be said that the question has not been raised again, for the practice has enjoyed peaceful and universal acceptance."[17]

20. (ii) The ability of Lutherans to adapt in matters of institutional order:

Luther saw nothing to prevent a woman from being able to exercise functions pertaining to the spiritual ministry. Because of their participation by baptism in the universal priesthood of believers, women have both the right and the equipment to proclaim the gospel and to administer the sacraments. But a woman cannot claim for herself this right because in accordance with the order of creation which finds expression in the natural law, she should be subordinate to man. Also she generally does not bring the natural capacities for this task. If a woman were to exercise

---

[14] Declaration, p. 7. The commentary is probably responding to the findings of a consultation of the Congregation with the Pontifical Biblical Commission which replied unanimously to it that "it does not seem that the New Testament by itself alone will permit us to settle in a clear way and once and for all the problem of the possible accession of women to the presbyterate". In addition the Pontifical Biblical Commission accepted by 12 votes against 5 "the view that scriptural grounds alone are not enough to exclude the possibility of ordaining women and that Christ's plan would not be transgressed by permitting the ordination of women". Cf. *Origins. National Catholic Documentary Service* (USA), July 1, 1976, p. 92–96.

[15] AAS 69, 101; Declaration, p. 5.

[16] Ibid.

[17] AAS 69, 101f.; Declaration, pp. 5f.

the preaching office in a congregation including men, she would act against the command that in the congregation "all things should be done decently and in order" (1 Cor 14 : 40). But in a congregation of women the woman would be quite suitable, in Luther's view, to exercise the spiritual ministry. The same could also happen in emergencies.[18] In the Lutheran churches this has become the usual position. For centuries women have been excluded from the spiritual ministry on the ground of "decency and order". But when this office was made accessible to women, it was done mostly by reference to the same apostolic command which had previously justified their exclusion. Another argument appealed to during the Second World War and afterwards was the emergency situation of congregations. The argument from tradition was also considered in discussions leading up to the innovation.

Not until 1929 did the Lutheran Church of the Netherlands first ordain women as pastors. It was followed by the Scandinavian churches which gave ordained women the full status of a pastor (Denmark 1947, Norway 1956, Sweden 1958). The German Lutheran churches have followed this example since the fifties, but without always entrusting to ordained women the complete range of pastoral functions. That evidences a symptom of hesitation within Lutheranism generally which has not disappeared everywhere even today.

21. (iii) The difficulties in simply and clearly identifying history and tradition:

If it is true that the uniform practice of the ancient and the medieval church makes any solemn declaration of the magisterium seem superfluous, then the difficulty surely arises of assigning an appropriate value to this practice. Looked at from the historical standpoint it is still not always possible to distinguish between the different motives behind this practice. For example, it is tied up with an androcentric approach, i.e., an anthropological view which was shared by the classic and most influential theologians such as Augustine and Thomas Aquinas. On this view women are related to men though the converse was never seriously taken into consideration, since men were held to be the exemplary gender of humankind. This anthropology was certainly not based on the revelation of God in Jesus Christ.[19] Gratian, the most influential Latin canonist, and

---

[18] Cf. Wilhelm Brunotte, *Das geistliche Amt bei Luther*, Berlin, 1959, pp. 193–199. — H. Lieberg, *Amt und Ordination bei Luther und Melanchthon*, Göttingen, 1962, pp. 60f., 79ff.

[19] On this anthropology, see K. E. Børresen, *Subordination and Equivalence. The Nature and Role of Woman in Augustine and Thomas Aquinas*, Washington, 1981.

Thomas Aquinas, the most representative medieval church doctor, give the same argument for their rejection of the ordination of women: "by her very nature, woman is in *statu subiectionis*".[20] Nor did the Reformation itself break with this anthropology. It is still unquestioned both in Luther and in later Lutheran theology. The same argument still underlies canon 968 of the Codex Iuris Canonici of 1917.[21]

History therefore provides no reliable access to the tradition in this present problematic. It is probably in this light that we must interpret the statement of *Inter Insigniores* to the effect that "in the final analysis it is the Church, through the voice of her Magisterium, that, in these various domains, decides what can change and what must remain immutable".[22]

22. C. The Symbolic Representation of Christ in His Ministers

(i) The question of the symbolic representation of Christ in the person who administers the sacrament is primarily a question of Catholic theology. This concept has been adopted in certain Lutheran theological circles, but it has met with radical criticism.[23] *Inter Insigniores* has two observations to make on this question:

The priest acts *in persona Christi capitis*, particularly in the celebration of the eucharist. According to the Scholastic logic of the sacramental sign: "When Christ's role in the Eucharist is to be expressed sacramentally, there would not be this 'natural resemblance' which must exist between Christ and his minister if the role of Christ were not taken by a man."[24]

A second observation is based on the symbolism of the salvation history in the same sacramental context. Christ assumed human nature in the male sex. This circumstance makes it possible for him to be the new Adam. Thus the covenant concluded by God with human beings appears

---

[20] Gratian, causa 33 qu. 3 cap. 11; Thomas Aquinas IV Sent. d. 25 qu. 2a. 1 ad. 1um. Cf. idem: "Cum... in sexu femineo non possit significari aliqua eminentia gradus... ideo non potest ordinis sacramentum suscipere."

[21] I. Raming, *The Exclusion of Women from the Priesthood; Divine Law or Sex Discrimination?* Scarecrow Press, Metuchen, N. J., 1976.

[22] AAS 69, 108; Declaration, p. 11.

[23] Thus e.g. Bishop Anders Nygren at the Church Synod in Sweden in 1957 (cited by M. Lindström, p. 49), although he did not vote for women's ordination. There is a penetrating criticism of the idea of representation in P. E. Persson, *Kyrkans ämbete som Kristusrepresentation*, Lund, 1961. Shortened German version: *Repraesentatio Christi. Der Amtsbegriff in der neueren römisch-katholischen Theologie.* Göttingen, 1966.

[24] AAS 69, 110; Declaration, p. 13.

like the mystery of marriage, just as Holy Scripture describes it (cf. Hos 1–3; Jer 3:1–13; Ezek 16:1–43, 59–63; Is 54:4–8; 62:4–5). The church therefore confronts Christ as the bride (Eph 5:21–32; Rev. 19:7–8). This leads to the statement that only a man can represent Christ in the celebration of the eucharist.[25]

23. (ii) The formula *in persona Christi* requires explanation:

The ambiguous interpretations which are offered of the formula *in persona Christi* make it essential that this formula be clarified because of the whole discussion of the ministry and not simply for the implications it has for the person of the minister.

a) In its original meaning, this formula gives expression to the fact that it is Christ and not the priest who accomplishes the sacrament.[26] This is a fine formulation, from an ecumenical point of view as well. In itself it does not imply that the priest must be a man.

24. b) On the other hand, if this formula identifies the priest too closely with Christ, it can lead to an unsatisfactory relationship of the role of the priest to the eucharistic assembly.[27] It is also essential to define carefully *in persona Christi* and *in persona ecclesiae*, i.e., to emphasize both the christological and the pneumato-ecclesiological dimension of the ordained ministry (see below No. 31).

25. c) The significance of the formula *in persona Christi* lies ultimately in the emphasis on the Christological dimension of the ministry. The Catholic effort to prevent any weakening of this dimension is a Christian concern.

---

[25] "And therefore, unless one is to disregard the importance of this symbolism for the economy of Revelation, it must be admitted that, in actions which demand the character of ordination and in which Christ himself, the author of the Covenant, the Bridegroom and Head of the Church, is represented, exercising his ministry of salvation — which is in the highest degree the case of the Eucharist — his role (this is the original sense of the word *persona*) must be taken by a man. This does not stem from any personal superiority of the latter in the order of values, but only from a difference of fact on the level of functions and service." AAS 69, 111f.; Declaration, p. 14.

[26] B. D. Marliangeas, *Clés pour une théologie du ministère. In persona Christi, in persona ecclesiae*, Théologie historique 51, Paris, 1978, especially p. 227.

[27] This direct identification of the priest with Christ is avoided by the epiclesis included in the new eucharistic prayers since the Second Vatican Council, which also points to the active role of the people. It should also be noted that in a quite general way an identification of priest and Christ was rejected by the Second Vatican Council to the extent that it never speaks of the priest as *alter Christus*. Ultimately the priest only represents Christ to the extent that on the basis of his ordination and his office he represents the faith and the communion of the church.

26. (iii) Finally it is of fundamental importance for our dialogue that reference should be made to the doctrinal caution of the above-mentioned declaration of the Congregation for the Doctrine of the Faith. It does not appeal emphatically to those points which refer to the symbolisation of representation but requires that this be viewed according to the analogy of faith.

III. THE ORDINATION OF WOMEN: A QUESTION WHICH GOES FAR BEYOND THE THEOLOGY OF MINISTRY

27. In the dialogue on the ministry as such, the question of the ordination of women appears to be an auxiliary question. Yet it becomes a very serious problem for our theological dialogue because it of necessity recalls the hermeneutic which we apply here. As we consider this, we indeed also, like it or not, take a stand on the status and role of Scripture and of tradition; the relationship between creation and eschatology, between Christology and pneumatology, and between the local church and the whole church. We also adopt a position on Mariology, on the relation of man and woman, and on the roots of Christianity in history. It is very important for our dialogue on the ordination of women to note that here, paradoxical as it may seem, at very least we make theological decisions about the nature of the ordained ministry itself.

A. Status and Role of Scripture and Tradition

28. In the Lutheran discussion on the relevance of biblical statements for the question of the ordination of women, a preeminent role has been placed by the distinction between what is historically conditioned and therefore changeable, and what is valid for all times and therefore unchangeable. Here it is the Confessions which serve as hermeneutical key.

In most of the churches which have accepted an ordination of women, the procedure has been to differentiate between the intention of the relevant Scripture passages and the concrete implementation of this intention in the particular social and cultural situations pertaining at any given time.[28] The unalterable intention of Scripture that everything should be done "decently and in order" (1 Cor 14:40) can therefore, it is argued, be implemented in different ways. Despite outward discontinuity, inner continuity can still be preserved. On this view, therefore, the introduction of the ordination of women cannot be regarded as a deviation from the

---

[28] For example, in the official report of the Bible Commission appointed by the Swedish Episcopal Conference, *Bibelsyn och bibelbruk*, Lund, 1970, pp. 35–46.

formal Reformation principle of *sola scriptura*. Yet there is no unanimity in the view taken on this question in the Lutheran churches.

29. On the Catholic side the problem of the ordination of women does not pose the question of the two sources of revelation. *Dei Verbum* No. 9 no longer sees the tradition as a source of revelation which in content would be different from Scripture: tradition is that which permits us to understand precisely its content.

On the Catholic side, therefore, the real problem is to know whether the formal uniformity of the tradition permits us with certainty to have access to the real content of revelation, and finally, whether real tradition arises out of simple repetition.[29]

B. The Connection of Creation and Eschatology

30. Respect for the order of creation in which, according to Paul, man is the head of woman, has been and still is invoked in both churches as an argument against the ordination of women. Yet even Paul holds that our present order is offset by the eschatological vocation of the baptized, as is explicitly stated in Gal 3:27-28. In the contemporary discussion witness to the coming world is offered as one of the theological grounds for the ordination of women. In this way, it is thought, men and women can bear witness in a society which is dominated by "sexism".

In the Decree on the Ministry and Life of Priests the Second Vatican Council connects the eschatological dimension of the ministry with the celibacy rule of Latin Catholicism because celibacy makes priests "a vivid sign of that future world" (Decree on the Ministry and Life of Priests, No. 16). In their priestly life they renounce a fundamental creaturely dimension, namely, marriage. In the Lutheran churches, on the other hand, the ordination of women could express the same eschatological dimension in a different form, namely, as an overcoming of sexual difference by sharing as partners in one sacred ministry.

The connection of the "dimension of creation" of the ordained ministry with its eschatological dimension is therefore a task common to us both.

---

[29] It must be affirmed, *pace* Vincent of Lerins: unanimously accepted and universally valid traditions which had been observed for a very long time by the church have been abandoned in the course of the years: for example, the treatment of post-baptismal sin in the early Church when only one reconciliation of the sinner was permitted; or the permitting of interest after it had been forbidden for 18 centuries. In addition to this, the tradition has an eschatological dimension which forbids its mere repetition. Could not Gal 3:27-28 also find an echo in the ministry?

C. The Connection of Christology and Pneumatology in the Ministry

31. The discussion about the connection of the roles of the minister, simultaneously that of being *in persona Christi* and that of being *in persona ecclesiae*, has shown the need to connect the christological and the pneumatological dimensions in the exercise of the ordained ministry.

If the *in persona Christi* is interpreted in isolation from pneumatology, this formula is not established in the ecclesia, the place of the communion of the Holy Spirit; we fall into a Christomonist and exclusively hierarchical view of the ordained ministry. Under these circumstances it is impossible to express the "we" of the Christians in the liturgy, in the responsibility of faith and life of the church. The ministers run the risk of being regarded directly as representatives of Christ with all the conflicts and unfortunate accompanying phenomena which follow.

But the ministry in particular should not be determined in an exclusively christological way; it should also be determined pneumatologically. That means establishing the specific charisma of ordination within the totality of the gifts which the Spirit gives to the church. Because they are the temple of the Spirit, the place of his gifts, the people can then become aware of themselves as the body of Christ having different members.

This connection of Christology and pneumatology is essential if we are to achieve a balanced view of faith which by its very nature is ecumenical.

Concretely it makes it possible:

— to establish the ministers in the church and not just over against it;

— to avoid the danger of any direct identification of the ministers with Christ;

— to permit a relationship to exist which is neither an ecclesial split nor an absorption in the church but one which represents an original and distinctive task which is to be carried out with constant reference to the faith and fellowship of the church, since this ministry can express the spirit and will of Christ;

— to secure for the "we" of Christians its place in the totality of the life of the ecclesia.[30]

---

[30] The sequence between chapters 2 and 3 of Lumen Gentium, the Dogmatic Constitution on the Church (Vatican II), Which assigns the minister his place within the church, pointed fundamentally in this direction. Have we allowed this its full weight? Also in the Lutheran tradition it is always necessary to heed the relation which exists between Confessio Augustana IV and V.

In face of a certain christological narrowing of our view of the ordained ministry, the relation between Christology and pneumatology is a problem confronting both Lutherans and Roman Catholics. Without thereby deciding the question of the ordination of women, a more consistent emphasis on the christological and pneumatological-ecclesiological dimensions of the ordained ministry would have a certain positive effect on the course of the discussion. Among other things, it would also relativise the question regarding the required "natural" likeness between Christ and the celebrant.[31]

D. The Connection between the Local Church and the Whole Church, or the Importance of Catholicity

32. For Catholics, ordained ministers are in a direct and preeminent way servants of the congregation, of unity among the local churches and therefore active bearers of catholicity. Their recognition is therefore essential. Even if the apostolic dimension of catholicity did not seem binding, it can nevertheless be predicted that there would be resistance to the introduction of the ordination of women so long as only a part of the Catholic Church of the West were in agreement with this step.[32] It is probable therefore that only an authority having the same weight as that of a universal council could make change possible in this area.

On the Lutheran side, the same concern for catholicity has a different importance; it can find expression in different ways in different places. It is assumed that the variety among the members of the church is integrated in one partnership of service, and only then could the ordination of Christian women become a sign of the essential catholicity of the local church.

E. The Place of the Virgin Mary in the Church

33. In the Roman Catholic Church the question of the ordination of women is sometimes linked with Mariology. For example, *Inter Insigniores* used the argument that the Virgin Mary received no office.[33] It is

---

[31] For the church fathers the fact that Christ was a man was not of particular interest. The situation is quite different in respect of Christ's being human, as the Creed confesses (humanity being common to both men and women). On this cf. R. A. Norris, "The Ordination of Women and the 'Maleness' of Christ", *Anglican Theological Review*, Supplementary Series 6, 1976, pp. 69–80.

[32] Prior to *Inter Insigniores*, official groups of Christians, women's orders, theologians, some bishops and even cardinals did not completely rule out the ordination of women. Cf. H. Legrand, "Views on the Ordination of Women", *Origins*, January 6, 1977, pp. 459–468.

[33] AAS 69, 103; Declaration, p. 7.

also sometimes asked in discussion whether the ordination of women is not especially advocated in the churches which allow only a small place for Mary in their religious life, or even none at all.

Yet it is not enough to emphasize the figure of Mary in order to achieve an equilibrium in the cooperation of men and women in the church. A new approach would only be achieved in this question if Mary is seen as a "model for all Christians, men and women" because of her "voluntary acceptance of the divine will".[34] An aspect which has only seldom been taken into account could then throw fresh light on the question of the ordination of women.

F. Importance of the Relation of Man and Woman

34. Is the question of the ordination of women only the tip of an iceberg, and of that which lies hidden beneath, namely the position which has always been assigned to women by a church which has become entangled in the structures of an androcentric society? Many object to this. But to clarify the controversy it will be important to overcome this androcentrism. Whether we ordain women or not, a considerable theological effort is required of our churches to analyse and remove the institutional, pedagogical, symbolic and linguistic effects (cf. the "sexist" language in the liturgy) of this androcentrism. This contribution is required of our churches for the common life of men and women.[35]

G. The Historical Roots of Christianity

35. In the view of some theologians, to support the ordination of women would contradict the historical origin of Christianity. The leadership of men in the eucharist is an expression of an historical "given" in the life of the church, quite remote from any form of gnosis. It corresponds to the fact that bread and wine are still used in the celebration of the eucharist even where they are not indigenous.[36]

---

[34] Paul VI, *Marialis Cultus*, AAS 68, 1976, p. 132.

[35] The liturgical commissions of the episcopal conferences in the English speaking countries have decided to eliminate all traces of sexist language from the liturgical texts. The American bishops conference voted in favour of changes in the liturgical texts as follows: "designed to eliminate from these liturgical texts anything that may be considered discriminatory to women" (Bishops' Committee on the Liturgy, *Newsletter* 17, 1981, p. 1). Cf. the similar recommendations of the LWF Assembly in Dar-es-Salaam (see note 2 above). Cf. the report of a Faith and Order Consultation, *Ordination of Women in Ecumenical Perspective*, op. cit., pp. 43–47 on "Male and Female Imagery".

[36] Ph. Delhaye, "Rétrospective et prospective des ministères féminins dans l'Eglise", *Revue Théologique de Louvain* 3, 1972, pp. 74–75.

H. Theological and Pastoral Significance

36. The ordination of women would affect not so much the theological significance of the ministry as its pastoral exercise. This seems to be paradoxical. Yet the ordination and the ministry of women would have to be in accordance with the same criteria of vocation and ordination as are in force in the case of men.

But pastorally there would be a real change, since the structure which has previously been shaped mainly by men would take a different shape in the case of a pastoral group composed of both men and women. Whether women are ordained or not, the establishment of a partnership of cooperation of this kind remains an important task in our churches.

IV. GENERAL CONCLUSIONS

37. (i) A divergence to be taken seriously and one which will continue for a long time:

The divergence in views about the ordination of women certainly does not coincide completely with the confessional boundaries between Lutherans and Catholics. Nevertheless the new order has scarcely any chance of entering into the Roman Catholic Church.

— In its authentic teaching, even if this is not solemn and binding doctrine, the Roman Catholic Church holds that "in fidelity to the example of its Lord" it "does not consider herself authorized to admit women to priestly ordination".[37]

— On the supposition that the Roman Catholic Church could change its conviction, which is unlikely, this would require a consensus of a kind which could only be produced by an authority equivalent to a universal council. It is also very unlikely that such a decision would be taken without consultation with the Orthodox sister church. All the prospects suggest that even if a change were possible at all, it could hardly be achieved in the foreseeable future.

If the divergence must be taken seriously and will certainly continue to exist for a long time, the question to be asked is whether its theological justification is irreversible on both sides.

---

[37] The semi-official commentary on *Inter Insigniores* considers a study of the ordination of women deacons (deaconesses) to be necessary. Cf. Documentation Catholique 59, 1977, 168. The results can be positive.

38. (ii) Theological justifications which could still develop:

Those who reject the ordination of women must recognize in respect of those who do it that this practice — contrary to appearances — cannot be explained exclusively by the pressure of the government on an established church or by feminist demands. Even if these secular factors have undeniably played a part, the Lutheran churches concerned have made the decision as a church to admit women to the ministry and in many cases after decades of theological reflection.[38] Contemporary practice is also scarcely to be compared with the gnosis of the early Church.

Discussion among Lutherans has shown that the same basic theological positions can lead to different practical conclusions. The shared concern that the church should live and act in accord with its original mission, has led, however, to the advocacy and to the rejection of the ordination of women on the basis of the same argument. Some reject the ordination of women in order to resist the accommodation of the church to a surrounding society which is influenced by feminism, which extends its secular principles to the sphere of the faith. Others practise the ordination of women precisely in order to resist accommodation to a society which, as in this case, is dominated by "sexism".

39. It can be stated quite generally that the churches which have introduced the ordination of women are not proposing any dogmatic or liturgical change in the ministerial office: women will assume the same ministry as the men. It is very unlikely, therefore, that the Lutheran churches will retrace their step. The new practice is indeed spreading and compels them to deepen their dialogue both domestically and with the Catholic Church. On the Catholic side it will be noted that the renewed endorsement of the non-ordination of women, addressed to all the faithful, has been clearly stated yet with considerable magisterial caution. In practice the formal authority which those responsible have chosen for *Inter Insigniores* (the declaration of a Congregation which has been confirmed by the Pope *in forma communi*) is relatively small. Such a choice seems to indicate that we are not dealing here with a doctrinally irreformable document.

In the contemporary situation of Catholic theology, this — theoretical — possibility of a change by the magisterium means that the ordination of women is not to be regarded as absolutely contrary to the Christian faith, even if the Catholic Church does not accept it for itself.

---

[38] In Sweden, for example, the question of the ordination of women was posed for the first time in 1923. But it was only in 1958 that a decision in favour was taken. See Martin Lindström, op. cit., pp. 10–21.

40. (iii) A question which shows the significance attached to a dialogue on theological hermeneutics:

As we have already seen, when we say "yes" or "no" to the ordination of women, we are not speaking merely of a special point in the theology of the ministry. That is too narrow a framework to deal properly with the problem. For precisely around this problem there crystallizes a whole set of questions of theological hermeneutics which call for treatment in their own right. It would be a great gain if these questions were to figure on the agenda of the Lutheran-Catholic dialogue, so as to speed up our progress.

41. (iv) The object of the ministry and the person of the minister:

The consensus which has been gained regarding the ordained ministry concerns its content and also its function. It is relatively independent of the decision (this depends on a more inclusive hermeneutic), which defines more closely who may exercise it. In good Lutheran as well as good Catholic theology, the question of the occupant of the office cannot push into the background the question of the content of the ministry.[39] This does not mean, of course, that the relation between the person of the minister and the content of the witness should be destroyed.

---

[39] This has been shown by L. M. Dewailly in "La personne du ministre ou l'objet du ministère", *RevScPhTh* 46, 1962, pp. 650–657. Dewailly approaches the question from a Thomist standpoint and his conclusions are similar to those reached by P. E. Persson in *Kyrkans ämbete som Kristusrepresentation* (op. cit.).

2.

One Mediator
by Yves Congar OP

Three themes or three expressions present problems in respect of the priestly office: the priest as mediator, the priest as *alter Christus*, the priest who acts *in persona Christi* and "represents" him.

Exaggerated statements can be found in the theological literature on all these themes; some of them are not only misleading but can even have a thoroughly repellent effect.

What Protestants fear is that an action of Christ be attributed to the person of the priest in the sense that he would of himself, in virtue of the power resident in him, produce the reality of grace, and that thus the present action of Christ and his Spirit would be abandoned. It is feared that the priest, by the capacity given to him by his ordination to act in the name of Christ, could become isolated from the church and that the priestly character of all believers and their capacity to approach God directly and freely could be denied (cf. Epistle to the Hebrews). All that would then remain for Christians would be a "second hand" religion.

The correct understanding of the formulae in question and where necessary the criticism and repudiation of certain interpretations are therefore very important.

Mediator

While recognizing that every Christian has direct access to God, it is right to point out that there is a ministry entrusted to certain persons by the church for the mediation of the gifts of God — Word and sacrament — and for intercession with God for human beings. It is in this sense that Thomas Aquinas speaks in Sum. Theol. III, q. 82, a 3. The Augsburg Confession (article V) and Calvin (Inst. IV, 3, 13) say the same thing, at least in respect of the ministerial mediation of God's gifts.

Evidence of an exaggerated and therefore completely misconceived view of the office of priest is found e.g. in the words of Anton Graf, professor of pastoral theology in Tübingen, who wrote in 1841: "According to generally accepted theological ideas, it is not God or Christ who act through the priest, but the priest himself who acts. The proclamation appears as his proclamation, the worship as his worship, the doctrine as his doctrine."[1]

---

[1] *Kritische Darstellung des gegenwärtigen Zustandes der praktischen Theologie*, Tübingen, 1841, pp. 106f.

Alter Christus

If this phrase meant that there are two "Christs", it would be a blasphemous or rather a foolish one. In actual fact, it means the precise opposite: Christ is the one and only one who brings salvation royally; the earthly ministers merely acquire significance as Christ is made visible through them. Within this general framework the formula has been used mainly in three contexts:

a) As an exhortation to express the responsibility of the priestly ministry and the spirituality which it requires.[2]

b) To describe what the priest should do; the equivalent as it were of *gerere personam Christi*.[3] The formula follows immediately a section which is cited in the Decree on the Ministry and Life of Priests of the Second Vatican Council;[4] but the Council itself does not use the term. In Pius X the reference to authority is confirmed: "Sacerdos... alter Christus vocatur et est communicatione potestatis".[5]

c) Finally the formula was used simply to describe priestly dignity.[6] The idea of the greatness of the priest also has been expressed in more questionable forms which Luther, too, criticised. For example, the priest stands above the angels and even above the Virgin Mary who brought Christ forth only once. — Exaggerated and sometimes ludicrous formulations of this kind affect our theme only marginally.

To speak of the priest as mediator makes sense to the extent that it means that the relation of the priest to Christ is the precondition of his existence, action and behaviour. He represents Christ for human beings. The danger

---

[2] For example, in the *Imitatio Christi* IV, 5, 3; in Tronson (cf. *Rev. Hist. Spiritualité* 51, 1975, pp. 73–98); Cardinal Mercier, *La vie intérieure*, Louvain, 1934, p. 161; Pius XII, *Adhortatio ad clerum* 23, IX, AAS 42, 1950, 659: veluti "alter Christus" and freq.; Msgr. Théas at the Second Vatican Council (*Doc. Cath.*, 1964, col. 1487); Paul VI to the pastors and Lent preachers, 11 February 1972 (*Doc. Cath.*, p. 205). Other texts can be found in the collection by Msgr. Veuillot, *Notre sacerdoce*, Paris, 2 vol., 1954.

[3] For example, Pius XI in the Encyclical *Ad catholici sacerdotii* of 20 December 1935 (DS 3755), in the section of this Encyclical which speaks of the dignity and nature of the priesthood.

[4] Walter M. Abbott, S. J. (general editor), *The Documents of Vatican II*, The America Press, 1966, Decree on the Ministry and Life of Priests, No. 12.

[5] *Exhortatio ad clerum catholicum* 1908 *Haerent animo*, AAS 41, 1908, 569.

[6] For example, in Manning, *La mission de l'Esprit-Saint dans les âmes.* Translated by R. MacCarthy, Paris, 1887, p. 381; and several Popes, including Pius XI, op. cit., DS 3755.

lies in the possibility that the original could be forgotten and all attention concentrated on the copy. — The formula *alter Christus* can be really disquieting. As we have seen, the Second Vaticàn Council avoided it although it had been recommended by a bishop, Msgr. Théas, and an American priest.[7]

Repraesentatio, gerere personam, in persona Christi

In the life of the church, especially at the celebration of the sacraments, the priest visibly plays the part of Christ.[8] The aim has been to express either (a) the aspect of visible representation or (b) the theological aspect of the effect produced by Christ who is represented in this way (not made present for he was never really absent, but represented visibly).

a) The priest *gerit figuram Christi*.[9] In the draft for the conciliar decree "De vita et ministerio sacerdotali" (as it was provisionally entitled) of 1964, No. 2, there was the formula "unum sacerdotium et ministerium Christi repraesentantes". When one of the council fathers sought to have the last word replaced by *participantes*, the Commission replied: "retinendam esse notionem repraesentationis; etenim de omnibus fidelibus vera ratione dicitur eos participare sacerdotium Christi quapropter notio participationis minus specifica est quam repraesentationis, quae multipliciter in Traditione exprimitur: sacerdos enim dicitur imago, typus, eikon, figura, etc. Christi Sacerdotis".[10] The term "share" or "participation" (*participatio*) was only rarely used in the new and final version of the Council's Decree on the Ministry and Life of Priests.

b) In Marliangeas' book[11] we find the expression or rather the list of occurrences of the expressions *in (ex) persona Christi, gerere personam (vocem) Christi, in nomine Christi* of Thomas Aquinas[12] and of Pius XII

---

[7] Th. Falls, Philadelphia, 27 October 1965, *Doc. Cath.*, 1966, col. 346.

[8] On this cf. above all: P. E. Persson, *Repraesentatio Christi. Der Amtsbegriff in der neueren römisch-katholischen Theologie*, Göttingen, 1966 (translation and excerpt from the Swedish original on which L. M. Dewailly has written an important critique in French. Cf. *Rev. Sc. Phil. Théol.* 46, 1962, 650–657. W. Breuning, "Amt und geschichtliche Kirche, Probleme der lehramtlichen Aussagen über das Priestertum", *Catholica* 24, 1970, 37–50. P. J. Cordes, "Sacerdos alter Christus". Der Repräsentationsgedanke in der Amtstheologie, *Catholica* 26, 1972, 38–49.

[9] Thomas Aquinas, IV Sent. d. 24 q. 1 q. 2 q.ª 1, obj. 3.

[10] De vita et ministerio sacerdotali, 1964, No, 2 E.

[11] B. D. Marliangeas, *Clés pour une théologie du ministère, In persona Christi. In persona Ecclesiae*. Preface by Y. Congar, Beauchesne, Paris, 1978.

[12] Ibid., pp. 143–146.

and the Second Vatican Council[13]. What is meant is quite plain: What the priest is because of his office, especially in the celebration of the sacraments, must be attributed to Christ as the source of this office. Instead of *in persona Christi*, Thomas Aquinas sometimes says *in virtute Christi*.[14] Charles Journet describes this accurately but not very elegantly, as "médiation de suppôt, immédiation de vertu" (*mediatio suppositi, immediatio virtutis*). Someone else (the priest) acts but in virtue of no other power than that of Christ. In this connection reference is also made to an "instrumental cause", the cause which bestows what it does not have and what does not derive from itself.

Significance of this Theology

What this reminds us of, above all, is the biblical theme of the *shaliah*: the ambassador represents the one who sends him; see the well known passage in the Apology of the Augsburg Confession: "They do not represent their own persons but the person of Christ, because of the church's call, as Christ testifies (Luke 10:16), 'He who hears you hears me.'"[15] Here as in Luther's Merseburg speech, it is quite clearly the act of preaching, of proclamation which is meant.[16] The significance of representation by the ambassador is set forth by H. Riesenfeld[17]. This is admissible even if we must go further, namely to a sacramental view of the church and, what derives from this, the theology of the church as the body of Christ, or, more specifically as the (visible) earthly body of the crucified and glorified Lord. Through the Holy Spirit a unity and solidarity of life exists between Christ and the church. When therefore the Lord, who is Spirit, works directly in human souls, he also makes use of materially perceptible and institutional means in which he himself becomes invisibly and sovereignly active. Priests, sacraments, and words are earthly forms of expression and means.[18]

Between the Roman Catholic Church and the Orthodox Church there is broad agreement on this theology, this view of the sacrament of the consecration of priests.[19] Even the theme of the priest as ikon, as image of

---

[13] Ibid., pp. 231–244.

[14] Ibid., p. 129.

[15] Apology of the Augsburg Confession, VII, 28; The Book of Concord, p. 173.

[16] WA 51, 15.

[17] H. Riesenfeld, *Das Amt im Neuen Testament*, VIII, pp. 125–172; *Unité et diversité dans le Nouveau Testament*, Lectio divina 98, Paris, Cerf, 1978.

[18] Marliangeas, op. cit., Y. Congar, Preface.

[19] Cf. findings of the Orthodox-Roman Catholic Consultations in the USA, *Doc. Cath.*, 7 Nov. 1976; *Irenikon* 49, 1976, No. 4, pp. 545–549.

Christ in the celebration of the liturgy, the idea that he acts *in persona* (=*in nomine*) *Christi*, is confirmed by the Orthodox.[20]

Difficulties, Objections, Dangers

The questions which follow are not put to us merely by our Protestant friends; we put them to ourselves. Contemporary reflection on the priestly ministry, on the other ministries and on ecclesiology equally raises these questions.

a) One section of Catholic dogmatic literature attributes to the priest, in virtue of the sacrament of orders, a new and profound likeness to Christ, the Priest, King and Prophet. The Reformers opposed this when they distinguished between a (universal) priesthood and the ministry, i.e., "having been born a priest through Baptism, a man thereupon receives the office; and this is what makes a difference between him and other Christians"[21]. For us, the consecration of priests is a sacrament and indeed, a sacrament with a "social" character which relates to the church as body. It bestows a special gift of grace and creates a structured reality within the body of the church. But the fact that the priests "differ from one another in essence and not only in degree", as Pius XII and the Dogmatic Constitution on the Church put it,[22] must be correctly interpreted. It means that the participation of the priest and the participation of all baptized believers in the priesthood of Christ are two different things. They cannot be placed on one and the same plane, namely, that of Christian existence as such; for that would turn the priest into a super-Christian. The priesthood of the baptized consists in their existence as Christians; the priesthood of the ordained ministry consists in a quality of ministry. It is also in this way that we have to interpret the formula of Pius XII who described the priest as *superiorem populo*.[23] This is precisely the case in the eucharistic action.

b) When we emphasize the special character of the priest in direct and exclusive dependence on Christ, we run the risk of no longer being able satisfactorily to reconcile the *in persona Christi* and the *in persona*

---

[20] Cf. Anthony Bloom in Y. Congar, Preface, Marliangeas, op. cit., p. 10; André Scrima, *L'Esprit Saint et l'Eglise*, Paris, 1969, p. 115; Anglican-Orthodox Report, No. 27, *Istina*, 1979, p. 73.

[21] Luther on Psalm 110, WA 41, 209; Luther's Works, American Edition, vol. 13, p. 332.

[22] Vatican II, Dogmatic Constitution on the Church, No. 10.

[23] Mediator Dei, DS 3250.

ecclesiae. The first becomes isolated from the second. But if, without mistaking the truth, we see the *in persona Christi* in the *in persona ecclesiae*, then the situation is different. Instead of a vertical, purely christological relationship (*Christomonism*) we deal with a trinitarian one, and thus the *vota fidelium* and the epiclesis are seen in their true light. Current reflections on the theology of the priesthood — in pneumatology and in ecclesiology — are moving in this direction, and this is very promising.

c) The Catholic position on the theme of the sacrament, but also on the position of the priest in the church, can conceal the danger of a tendency towards automatism. The "power" given by God to the priest can be assigned such a place and such efficacy that the priest, instead of being simply a representative, becomes an arbitrary substitute. The passage cited by Mirbt from the Catechismus Romanus (in other respects a fine document) could illustrate that: "Quum episcopi et sacerdotes tanquam Dei interpretes et internuncii quidam sint, qui eius nomine divinam legem et vitae praecepta homines edocent, et ipsius Dei personam in terris gerunt..."[24] What the priest does and says would thus be guaranteed ipso facto as coming from God. Fundamentally this is what P. E. Persson objects to; a standpoint which makes "the *what* depend on the *who*". We have come across the following position in Thomas Stapleton, one of the extreme exponents of the Counter Reformation: "in doctrina fidei, non quid dicatur, sed quis loquatur a fideli populo attendendum est"[25].

If I am not mistaken, the Reformation theology of the Word of God here plays a decisive role, together with Luther's principle "non sacramentum, sed fides sacramenti". The Reformers were concerned to ensure that there should be no automatism or any attribution of efficacious grace to a creaturely power, but rather a realization of the promise of God through the proclaimed word.

Conclusion

The aim of the Reformation was to replace a world of hierarchically ordered ontological attributes by a universe of personal relationships. It therefore worked against a scholasticism which in the end was abandoned to its domestic quarrels. During and after the Second Vatican Council the efforts of the Roman Catholic Church were largely directed to extricate itself from this scholasticism and to follow the yearning for what may be

---

[24] Mirbt/Aland, *Quellen zur Geschichte des Papsttums und des römischen Katholizismus*, J. C. B. Mohr, Tübingen, 1967, p. 683, 1056.

[25] *De principiis fidei doctrinalibus*, 1572, lib. X, chap. V.

defined, without unrealistic idealism, as the undivided church. The priesthood appeared here:

1. As a real function based on a gracious appointment. By grace the priest is equipped to act, i.e., to exercise a ministry in the name and by the power of Christ.[26]

2. As activity in a community for the service of which the priest is consecrated, a community which is not passive but, quickened by the Spirit and rich in gifts of the Word and charismata, constitutes with the priest in an organic way the subject of all sacred actions: life of faith, apostolate, diaconia and charity, liturgy...

---

[26] Vatican II, Decree on the Ministry and Life of Priests, Nos. 5 and 7: "Through the ministry of the bishop, God consecrates priests so that they can share by a special title in the priesthood of Christ. Thus, in performing sacred functions they can act as the ministers of Him who in the liturgy continually exercises his priestly office on our behalf by the action of His Spirit."

(The original text is in French.)